WE ARE THE SACRED MASCULINE RISING

8 MEN SHARE THEIR STORIES OF GROWTH, HEALING, AND SPIRITUAL AWAKENING

BRIAN CORMACK CARR   BRIAN MATZKE
DANIEL T. EDWARDS   MATTY RYCE   MICHAEL DOYLE
RANIN - RAWA   TIMOTHY ALEXANDER
ZACHARY HARDING

SOULFULLY ALIGNED PUBLISHING

Copyright © 2021 by Soulfully Aligned Publishing

All rights reserved. Apart from any fair dealing for the purposes of research or private study, or criticism or review, as permitted under the Copyright, Designs, and Patents Act 1988, this publication may only be reproduced, stored, or transmitted, in any form or by any means, with the prior permission in writing of the copyright owner, or in the case of the reprographic reproduction in accordance with the terms of licensees issued by the Copyright Licensing Agency. Enquires concerning reproduction outside those terms should be sent to the publisher.

CONTENTS

Introduction	v
1. Brian Cormack Carr	1
ACES High: How to Play Your Best Hand in Life	
About the Author	21
2. Brian Matzke	23
Broken Open: A Spiritual Awakening & Journey Through PTSD	
About the Author	43
3. Daniel T. Edwards	44
Escape the Rat Race & Live life on your Terms NOW!	
About the Author	61
4. Matty Ryce	63
You Are The Answer	
About the Author	79
5. Michael Doyle	80
The Journey Inward: The Not So Obvious Path to Self-Mastery	
About the Author	97
6. Spiritual Name: Ranin-Rawa	99
Government Name: Geoff Larden	
About the Author	119
7. Timothy Alexander	120
Time to Rise	
About the Author	128
8. Zachary Harding	129
From DJ to CEO – A guide to better decision-making skills	
About the Author	141
9. About the Publisher	143

INTRODUCTION

Masculinity is a loaded word. Too often, and for too long, it has been linked with hetero-normative dominance, colonial power, and destructive patriarchies. For too many people in the world, it signals less 'power with' and more 'power over': power over women; nature; history; the economy; our planet; indigenous communities; the young; the old; and other men. This is the prevailing culture of toxic masculinity—an insatiable, unsustainable masculine concept that harms everyone and everything (including itself) as it rapaciously feeds on the true potential of all who fall under its shadow.

There is another, better way.

There is the possibility of a *tonic* masculinity. One that embraces difference and diversity. One that cultivates, shepherds and shares the world's bountiful resources in ways that are sustainable and ethical. One that guides and uplifts the young, empowering them to rise in truth and love. One that venerates its soul-partner, the Feminine. One that spreads not shadow, but light—a life-enhancing light that enables all who are touched by it to flourish.

The men who have created this book believe deeply in this vision of masculinity. They feel it in their very souls. They stand for true, life-giving masculinity. Inclusive, balancing masculinity. *Sacred masculinity.*

We Are The Sacred Masculine Rising explores:

• The possibility that all men may live their lives in mutually-supportive freedom;

• The opportunity to alchemise the distorted masculine into a unified masculine;

• The journey inward that can gift every man with the power of self-love and divine self-worth beyond all worldly expectations;

• Every man's innate ability to transcend deep trauma and to blossom into the healthy, whole identity that is his birthright.

In the pages that follow, you will meet men from a variety of backgrounds, with a variety of life experiences. We are coaches, healers, entrepreneurs, entertainers, and activists. We are also ex-cops, ex-firefighters, and ex-drug dealers. We are DJs, and we are CEOs. We are you.

Join us, as we share details of our individual journeys from lostness to redemption; addiction to recovery; separation to reconciliation; illness to healing; bereavement to transcendence; and duality to wholeness. Listen, as we share our understanding that *true* masculinity is everything it ever was, and everything it could never be before this moment in time.

We are the hunter; the gatherer; the farmer; the warrior; the healer; the hurt; the shaman; the witch; the priest; the father; the son; the brother; the master; the servant; the partner; the doctor; the nurse; the strong; the vulnerable; the man; the boy; the one-who-has-a-stiff-upper-lip; the one-who-wears-his-heart-on-his-sleeve; the steely; the sensitive; the achiever; the nurturer; the athlete; the king; the queer; the thinker; the doer; the active; the passive; the rugged; the fey; the-one-who-laughs; the-one-who-cries; the extrovert; the introvert; the vocal; the quiet; the rough; the gentle; the brave; the timid; the gay; the straight; the cis; the trans; the man-in-touch-with-his-inner-female; the-female-in-touch-with-her-inner-male; the one who defies all gender boundaries; the Yang-who-dances-with-Yin; the blue; the pink; the rainbow; the celebration of difference; the transcendence of opposites; the absolute equal and complement to the Sacred Feminine; the understanding and certainty that we are all ultimately One.

We Are The Sacred Masculine Rising, and we extend to you our hands and our hearts in loving welcome.

Brian Cormack Carr

1

BRIAN CORMACK CARR

ACES HIGH: HOW TO PLAY YOUR BEST HAND IN LIFE

INTRODUCTION

You are a genius. You may not believe it, but you are.

I don't mean in the modern sense of *exceptionally intelligent*—although you may be that, too. I mean in the original, Latin sense of *an innate ability or inclination*, and *the attendant spirit present from one's birth*.

I mean in the sense of your very essence.

Unfortunately for most of us, our culture does a great job of squashing geniuses. From birth onwards, often for very commendable reasons—and by people who feel responsible for us, like our parents, our teachers, our employers, and even the government—we're taught to toe the line. To fit in. To *be sensible*. We're taught that we are vulnerable bags of blood and bone blundering about in a dangerous universe, and that the most important thing for us to do is to find security. To settle down. To play it safe. To ignore our unrealistic dreams.

That approach isn't all bad, of course—we need food in our bellies and a roof over our heads, after all—but it's a very partial picture, and it can create *major* problems for us further down the line. After all, what price safety? What happens when we look around and hate the roof that we've been building above us all our lives? What happens when we climb the ladder of ambition and achievement and realise —often too late, and to our great horror—that it has been leaning against the wrong wall?

Here's the thing: what you ultimately are is *not* a vulnerable bag of blood and bone blundering about in a dangerous universe. You *are* that universe, expressing itself. You are creation in motion, and you have a unique place to fill and a specific purpose to unfold in this world. You know this, don't you? (Spoiler alert: discovering this fact is your *ultimate* purpose, but there are some interesting staging posts along the way.)

I know you. You're tired of pretending to be limited when, deep down, you know you're unlimited. You're weary of the strain of acting small when, deep down, you know that you're actually vast. You know that you are called to serve and that you have something to offer the world, if only you could find it, articulate it, believe in it—and then figure out a way to share it.

Well, you can, and you're going to.

Join me as I share with you how I discovered that I am something greater than I thought I was—and that everyone and everything else is greater than I thought they were, too; and, how I discovered a simple, natural process that can put *you* in touch with that realisation. It's a journey into the imaginal realm of the collective unconscious; along the Royal Road of the archetypes; and into the very depths of creation. It's a journey into you and me, and the potential that lies inside all of us, just waiting patiently to be unfolded. It's an invitation to play the hand that life has dealt you, in the brilliant way that only *you* can play it. It begins with a death, a dream, and a deck of cards...

I. A DEATH

When I was nine years old, my mother died, and everything changed.

She had been becoming progressively sicker for the previous two years from an extremely rare and aggressive form of a blood disorder called Primary Plasma Cell Leukaemia. This cancer is characterized by the out-of-control growth of a particular type of immunity-supporting white blood cell. In effect, it results in a part of the immune system—that amazing God-given servant that helps keep us safe from infection and illness—turning on its host. It had a very poor prognosis then, and even now, nearly forty years later—and despite considerable advances in medical science—it still has a poor prognosis.

If God wanted to deal you a one-in-a-million hand that ensured that your life would change completely, irrevocably, and forever—this would fit the bill.

Mum's death did change my life, and in more ways than one. It was a terrible blow, of course—but rather than knocking me out, it knocked me *open*. It enabled me to discover (or perhaps, rediscover) a level of reality I may not have found easily otherwise. As Joni Mitchell sings, "something's lost but something's gained in living every day".

Of course, I didn't know this at the time. All I knew back then was that Mum was becoming weaker, paler, quieter, and more and more tired with every day that passed. I knew that she couldn't do some of the 'normal' things that she used to be able to do and that my friends' mothers could still do—like helping on school trips and sports days, or playing rough-and-tumble games, or tucking me into bed at night. I knew that she was becoming further away from me with every day that passed: literally, as she became gradually house- and then bed-bound; and metaphorically, as she receded further and further into herself.

Towards the very end of her life, I saw her appearance change dramatically. She lost all of her hair and all of her teeth, and the whites of her eyes turned completely red as her capillaries gradually disintegrated.

She was dissolving, right in front of me. But to me, she was still my beautiful Mum.

My parents never told me that she was going to die—a fact for which I'll be eternally grateful. I can't know how I would have reacted had I been told, of course; but I recognize that there's every chance I would have been terrified, hysterical, maybe even angry—and perhaps even at them. It's possible I would have tried in vain to cling on to what couldn't be clung on to. As it was, I simply loved her and tried to make her feel as well as I could, moment-by-moment-by-moment. I seemed to know, deep down, that that was the right thing to do; that that was the only thing I *could* do.

The last time I saw her, we were both in my dad's car. I was being dropped off at my grandmother's house for the night, and Dad was taking Mum to hospital for one of the regular blood transfusions that were, by that point, all that kept her alive.

The last thing we said to each other as I hopped out of the car, giving her a quick kiss as I went, wasn't "goodbye", but "I love you".

II. A DREAM

Although I wasn't told Mum was dying, deep down, I knew. In fact, the knowledge of what was happening came to me in a dream some months before she passed.

In the dream, I sat in a beautiful theatre. The seats were framed in gilded baroque moulding and upholstered in plush red velvet, and the same red velvet formed the heavy curtains which draped thickly in crimson tumbles at either side of the stage. I was the only person in the audience, and all was silent. As the lights dimmed, a spotlight shone onto the stage, and from its right-hand side, a beautifully ornate open-topped carriage began to move slowly into view. I could see nothing pulling it—invisible horses, perhaps—but it glided silently from right-to-left across the stage.

On the carriage sat a queen. She wore robes of silver and gold that shimmered as though made of moonlight, and on her head was a crown arrayed in enormous, glowing stars. Her head was larger than the rest of her, and so her face became the focus of my attention. It was a face I recognised. Mum.

She was smiling, beautiful, and healthy. She didn't speak; but as the carriage slowly made its way towards the left-hand side of the stage, she looked directly into my eyes, and waved to me. She was beaming, happy, peaceful. She continued waving, smiling beatifically at me from beneath her crown of brilliant stars, and gradually disappeared into the wings at the other side of the stage. I woke up.

Although I couldn't have articulated it in words at the time, the dream transmitted particular knowledge to me: it told me that my mum was dying and that she would soon be leaving this world forever. It told me that, at a deeper level of existence, and behind the form in which Mum was appearing to me in 'real life', she was fundamentally okay. More than okay—she was perfect. And it told me that, at a deeper level of existence, behind the form of the sad, scared little boy that I believed myself to be, so was I.

The ultimate message was this: *That which you really are is eternally safe.*

There were other messages in there too: Life is but a dream. God speaks to us in symbols. Forms are never a reality. All forms must fade. What is real is beyond form. What is real is Love. Love is never lost.

It has taken me a lifetime to integrate these messages.

III. A DECK OF CARDS

It might surprise you to know that, despite this early traumatic experience, I consider myself to have had an extremely happy and stable life and even a happy childhood. After Mum died, my extended family—my grandmother and aunts and uncles—rallied around and supported me and Dad. My amazing dad—who told me not long after we lost Mum, "I'll just have to be your mum as well as your dad now, and we're going to get through this together"—did a brilliant job of supporting me through my grief and giving me as normal and secure a childhood as possible in the circumstances.

A couple of years later, he remarried. My brief moments of concern at the prospect of having a 'new mum' quickly dissipated when I first met his then lady friend (strangely enough, my first sight of her was when she got into the car and sat in the very same place I had last seen my mum). I liked her immediately, and things only got better from there. We quickly formed a strong bond and a happy family unit. I had a new Mum, after all—and I still do.

Some people are lucky if they are gifted with one good parent. How blessed with riches am I to have received three? I'm the little boy who lost his mother, but who has never—not for one single second of life—been motherless. Love never skipped a beat, and I'm glad I noticed that.

All forms must fade. What is real is beyond form.

My journey into adulthood was pretty average after that. I enjoyed school, and did well there, making friends and getting good grades. I left to go to university in Aberdeen to study English Literature and Language and, despite a shaky first term—I had a horror of being separated from my parents for too long, a throwback to what had gone before, I suppose—I enjoyed my time there, too. And I did well. I left with an honours degree in English Literature and Language, and entered the world of work, apparently well set-up for success.

Before I get to that part of the story, though, I need to tell you about the deck of cards, and how it relates to *that* dream.

In my first term at university, I became friends with a girl in my hall of residence who had a deck of tarot cards. I had heard of the tarot, of course, but had never seen the cards up close. I was fascinated by them. We took turns reading for each other, using the accompanying guidebook to help us. I wasn't particularly struck by any sense of the cards' predictive ability—but I *was* struck by how well the readings helped me to clarify my thinking about things. (It's useful to have a means of clarifying one's thinking about things when one is a young, hormonal, gay-but-still-in-the-closet boy on the cusp of adulthood, living away from home for the first time in his life.)

I was also struck by how the cards seemed to speak to universal truths. I could *sense* that there was a deeper reality behind their symbolic, dream-like images.

I became so enchanted by the cards, I bought myself a deck. I also started reading about the history of tarot. Before long, I learned of what has become the world's most popular tarot deck: the Rider Waite-Smith Tarot, first published in 1909. This was created by Arthur Edward Waite, and the artist Pamela Coleman Smith, who— along with such famous luminaries as the poet William Butler Yeats and such notorious mischief-makers as the occultist Aleister Crowley

—were two members of the London-based magical order, the Hermetic Order of the Golden Dawn.

In looking through my first copy of the Waite-Smith deck, I was particularly drawn to the twenty-two lavishly-illustrated Major Arcana cards, which depict powerful universal and archetypal forces. They start with the Fool, which depicts an androgynous figure stepping towards a cliff-edge, head held high, holding a white rose. Then comes the Magician, who has one arm up and one arm down, channeling divine power into the mundane world, his magical implements, and the symbols for the four suits of the tarot—the wand, the cup, the sword, and the pentacle—set before him on his table. Then we have the High Priestess, who gazes inscrutably towards us as she sits in front of a gossamer-thin veil draped between ornate white and black marble columns, her blue and grey robes tumbling to her feet where they foam like waves. Then the Empress, who sits on—

I stopped short when I got to the Empress. I had seen this image before. The shimmering robes. The carriage-like seat. The crown of glowing stars. Facing this time, not towards stage left, but stage right —as though entering, rather than leaving, the scene. It was the image from my dream.

Of the Empress card, Arthur Edward Waite says, in his *Pictorial Key to the Tarot (1911)*:

A stately figure, seated, having rich vestments and royal aspect, as of a daughter of heaven and earth. Her diadem is of twelve stars, gathered in a cluster. The symbol of Venus is on the shield which rests near her. She is... the fruitful mother of thousands... She is, above all things, universal fecundity and the outer sense of the Word... The card of the Empress signifies the door or gate by which an entrance is obtained into this life, as into the Garden of Venus; and then the way which leads out therefrom, into that which is beyond...

What is real is beyond form.

IV. IS REAL LIFE OVERRATED?

Back to my story. I left university and, being sure of nothing other than that I didn't want to be a schoolteacher, I started applying for jobs. I soon got a very good one, as a graduate trainee manager for Marks and Spencer. I completed my training and moved into personnel management, where I quickly found my leadership style—one that was coaching-based and focused on helping employees find their gifts and solutions to everyday work challenges.

However, I wasn't happy. It wasn't that I hated the job. The problem was that I didn't *love* it. It didn't feel like *me*. Somehow, I just couldn't get excited about store profit and loss accounts, salary reconciliations, share growth, or the sales figures for men's hosiery. I wanted to be of service to the world, and I knew I needed to find another route.

I found my way—via a brief stint in children's social work and a whole host of voluntary work positions—to the charity sector, where I remain to this day (I'm chief executive of a charity which supports voluntary action in local communities). Here, I was able to work with like-minded people, to share my gifts, to make a positive difference, to raise millions of pounds for programmes that support (and continue to support) many disadvantaged groups—in other words, to truly *serve*.

I was also able to further refine my true calling, which is coaching, and teaching others to coach. In 2009 I developed my own coaching practice as a side-line. This was partly to fulfill what I came to call my *vital vocation*—which became the title of my first coaching book—and partly to protect myself against the post-recession vagaries of the job market. It was a heady time. I coached business and private clients including government advisors. I trained coaches. I wrote two bestselling books. I was hired by the Franklin Covey organisation to deliver their flagship '7 *Habits of Highly Effective People*' programme. I was fulfilled at last—well, pretty much. There still seemed to be something *missing*. A gap. An absence. Something

I wasn't seeing. A feeling that I wasn't yet holding all the cards. What was it?

It took another death to show me.

V. THE CRACK THAT LETS THE LIGHT IN

My Dad died last year, at the start of the coronavirus pandemic; not from Covid, but from cancer. Despite my living some four hundred miles away—he in Scotland, me in England—I was able, with the permission and support of his doctors, to travel back home to be with him and Mum during his final days.

To have been with him throughout that time; to have said a last goodbye (this time, I knew consciously that a leaving was imminent); to have helped care for him in those final hours; to have been able to hold his hand as he took his last breath: these were the privileges of my life.

In the days that followed Dad's death, and despite the ongoing lockdown, the world seemed strangely alive. I went for walks in the town and countryside near my parents' house, and everything, both animate and inanimate, shone with light and vibration. It was as though I was seeing *behind* everything, and into its very essence. The sky. The trees. The birds. The barley waving in the fields. The buildings. The cigarette butt in the gutter at the side of the road.

This time, I didn't need a dream to speak to me of the continuous, unbroken, spaceless, timeless reality of who and what we really are. It was evident all around me. It had been evident in the care, and the tears, and the pain, and the grief, and the loss, and the light. It was evident then, and it's still evident now. Things don't happen *to* us, but *for* us. The things we think are outside us are in fact our very self.

We are Love, disguised as people.

This was what was missing. I needed to coach people not simply to be better or to achieve more, but to connect with their true nature. To connect with it, unfold it, live it, and bring its bountiful gifts into this world that needs them so badly.

Then, ACES arrived and brought me full circle.

VI. ANOTHER GIFT FROM WITHIN

It was a few months after Dad's death. I had been asked to speak at a tarot conference on the topic of manifesting goals. It was a welcome distraction. I decided I would speak about the coaching model that I had been trying to develop, on-and-off, for several years. The only problem was, I hadn't figured out *exactly* what that model was. I knew it was inside me, but it was less of a solid framework, and more of an impressionistic *feeling*. I hadn't really been able to fully articulate it, and to do so would involve considerable work, I thought.

What I *did* know was that it—like most good coaching models—would have several stages. There would be a stage that explored the context of the client's goals and ambitions. There would be a stage in which the client discerned and decided which course of action to follow. There would be a stage in which the client moved forward, turning plans into actions, and facing and overcoming obstacles. And there would be a stage in which the client received and reviewed their results and—if necessary—recalibrated before taking their next steps.

As I sat jotting down notes on this possible model, I noticed my deck of Waite-Smith Tarot cards sitting nearby. I picked it up and began shuffling and sorting through it, meditatively, as I often do when I need to think. I wasn't going to read the cards; just the gentle shuffling and sorting would be enough to clear my mind.

Shuffle, shuffle, shuffle.

The familiar images flickered past my eyes. The Fool. The Chariot. The Three of Pentacles. The Six of Swords. The Knight of Wands. Death. Temperance. Justice. And of course, my beautiful Empress.

Suddenly, and as though being moved from a place beyond myself, I felt compelled to pull out the Aces and to arrange them in front of me in a very specific order: The Ace of Cups; the Ace of Swords; the Ace of Wands; the Ace of Pentacles.

In the Waite-Smith deck, each Ace depicts a huge hand emerging from tumultuous clouds looming above the landscape, proffering the relevant suit's emblem. As I gazed at the cards, I realised that each one represented a different stage in the four-stage coaching model that was beginning to emerge from inside me.

- The Ace of Cups (elementally related to Water, and the human heart) suggested the pouring forth of *awareness*, of 'that which is given', the very ground of our being and the raw life material we have to work with.

- The Ace of Swords (elementally related to Air, and the human mind) suggested our moment-by-moment ability to *choose* how to respond to what faces us.

- The Ace of Wands (elementally related to Fire, and the human drive, or libido) suggested the process of putting *energy* and work into the thoughts and actions necessary to move forward in any given situation.

- Finally, the Ace of Pentacles (elementally related to Earth, and corporeal reality) suggested the tangible results of our efforts—results which, through acceptance and gratitude, could provide us with new material to work with. Our next gift. A new awareness to *surrender* to.

Then—in what was a very thrilling moment—I realised what each of these stages spelled out: Awareness. Choice. Energy. Surrender.

A... C... E... S.

ACES!

It fit perfectly, both with my coaching work, and my tarot work. I realised that this *was* the process I had been using, and had been guiding my clients and students to use, for many years. I just hadn't realised how naturally and organically it all fit together as a process, and how powerfully *deep* it actually was. This wasn't just a coaching model—it was a description of the way in which we each create our own reality, moment-by-moment-by-moment.

The ACES Manifestation Methodology was born, and I had received another gift, from—what? From whom? Perhaps, from the archetypal energy that manifests in the tarot deck; and in the dreams of sad, scared little boys; and in Life itself.

VII. THE ACES METHODOLOGY

Since that moment, I have coached clients through ACES (as you'll see in a moment, it's a cycle, perhaps even a spiral) and I have taught many other coaches, consultants, therapists and tarot readers to use it with their own clients too—most recently in my popular online training course, *Tarot Coach Session Success.*

"It's the most empowering reading I've had. Sometimes I walk away from my tarot cards feeling as though I just have to wait for fate to unfold. I walked away from the coaching session with you feeling like I had a specific part to play."
– Tarot student

"ACES really helped me organise my thinking and my plans. I even got myself a tarot deck and carried the four Ace cards with me to remind me of the way in which the Universe was working to support me!"
– Coaching client

"I've started using ACES with my coaching clients. They are loving it, and so am I – it's so simple, yet so powerful. Co-creation is real!"
– Coaching student

ACES is a highly effective coaching (and self-coaching) approach, for a couple of very simple reasons. Firstly, it describes the way in which reality is created and is experienced by each of us in every moment of our lives; and secondly, it articulates the process by which we can engage with the development of that reality in a truly co-creative way.

Come with me on a short journey through ACES. It starts (and ends) with *Awareness*.

AWARENESS

Awareness is everything. There's nothing that it's not. Everything you've ever experienced (or ever will experience, or ever *could* experience); every thought you've ever thought (or ever will think, or ever *could* think); and every dream you've ever dreamed (or ever will dream, or ever *could* dream), arises in your awareness. Awareness has to exist first, before any of those other phenomena—things, thoughts, dreams, and even life events—can exist. Awareness is primary. Awareness is the very ground of being.

Even apparently physical happenings that seem to be independent of consciousness—like people, places, animals, plants, planets, historical periods, scientific discoveries, works of art, the weather— are only ever known to us through our *awareness*.

This part of the ACES process invites you to become aware of what arises in *your* awareness. What do you feel called to? What do you feel pulled towards? What do you feel repelled by? Here is the call of your 'attendant spirit', your unique genius. As my mentor, Barbara Sher (an expert career guide, called by some 'the godmother of life coaching') has said, *"What you love is what you are gifted at, and there are no exceptions"*.

She pointed out that the things we love reveal our talents, and our unique way of understanding things. This is the essence of Awareness. This is what your genius wants you to know. This is the hand that Life is dealing you. Are you listening?

COACH YOURSELF: AWARENESS

What do you love? Make a list, no matter how insignificant the items on that list may seem.

Do you see any patterns? Here is where it's time to employ the practices that allow you to get in touch with that awareness. Stillness. Silence. Meditation. Mindfulness. Listening. Letting yourself simply *be*.

What arises in your awareness? In your conscious mind? In your unconscious, through your dreams? In your heart of hearts? Listen carefully. Life *is* calling to you.

You might momentarily lose your awareness of the call; but you can never, ever lose the call of awareness itself.

It is *you*.

"I did what you recommended and kept a diary of all the things I noticed that provoked that 'love' response in me. Even the little things. None of them seemed all that significant at the time, but when I looked at my list, I could see the connections between them. Oh my God – I'm supposed to be an artist! How can I have forgotten that? I've enrolled in classes..."
– **Coaching client**

CHOICE

The second stage in ACES is both the simplest and the most challenging. Here lies the metaphorical fork in the road. Choice is about responsibility—or *response-ability*, our ability to respond to what we have become aware of. Will we be passive, or participatory? Will we engage, or look around for the nearest exit? Will we listen to and act upon our heart's desire, or push it back down into the depths? Will we stay awake, or go back to sleep?

Our one true freedom in this life is in recognising that, whilst we may not have control over what ultimately happens to us (life, after all, is bigger than any one individual) we *do* have a choice in how we respond to what is happening to us. As Zen teacher Cheri Huber says, *"the quality of your life depends on the focus of your attention"*.

COACH YOURSELF: CHOICE

I invite you now to attend to the two choices you can make at any given moment.

Firstly, you can choose to commit to taking an ongoing, co-creative role in the unfolding of your life, whatever is happening, and wherever that may lead you.

Secondly, you can choose what to focus your attention on in order to further the fulfillment of your goals and dreams.

Thoughts appear in your awareness, and you can choose which thoughts to believe, and which thoughts to question. Are you focused on the problems, or the path ahead? Are you focused on what scares you, or on the solutions to your fears?

In both cases, you'll find that truly focusing on the latter will dissolve the former.

"I got stuck in the assumption that I needed a particular qualification to work in teaching. I didn't realise I could find other ways to share my knowledge and expertise with people who need my support. By focusing on what I could do, I've managed to build a small list of IT students, and I'm getting great feedback on my mini-courses. It's a start!
– Coaching client

ENERGY

It is likely that you will spend more time here than in any other of the four stages of ACES. Consider this the *engine room* of ACES. Once we have our goals, we must put our energy into them—both in terms of ideas and in terms of action. This can include all manner of psychological, spiritual, and imaginative activities and methods—but it also *must* include concrete action steps and actual practical effort.

Of course, any course of action is likely to lead to the appearance of obstacles along the way. Obstacles are not to be feared. They are to be 'untangled'. To be worked with, moved around, stepped over—or to be acknowledged as signs that it's time to find a different path. In any event, obstacles are *always* useful—*if* we put them to our service, and learn from them.

COACH YOURSELF: ENERGY

At this stage, you can employ many different practices—anything that enables you to energise the things that support you, and to untangle the things that don't. It's a good idea to find your favourite energising methods and to employ them often.

Try consciously day-dreaming; goal-setting; creating milestones; employing productivity and motivational methods; using affirmations, vision boards, and rituals; finding support and accountability teams and mentors; applying inquiry-based stress reduction techniques.

Energise, untangle—and keep moving forward!

"I used to get stuck in such negative thinking. You helped me to not beat myself up for having negative thoughts. But now I know to write them down and to gently question them, and to try to find alternative perspectives and options. I'm now the 'solutions guy' rather than the 'problems guy', LOL"
– Coaching client

"My calendar is my new best friend. I plot everything in there, even rest periods (I'd forget to take them otherwise). And I've taken up Qi Gong. It helps keep me calm, even when things get super-busy. I don't feel guilty

about doing it, because I see it as part of my ACES practice. It's important – it's helping me move forward!'
– Coaching client

SURRENDER

This stage brings us full circle. Life happens—have you noticed? Things manifest in our awareness, and after a time, new things manifest. Will they be the things we thought we wanted to manifest, or something else entirely?

Believe it or not, both outcomes are fine, and exactly as they should be. There is no mistake in this present moment. It is what it is. We can plan, prepare, work hard, train, visualise, focus, affirm our intentions, mould our mindset, cross our 'i's, dot our 't's, and get all our lovely little ducks in a row—all practices that definitely have value—and ultimately, we get what we get in the moment we get it. That's just how life works. What is, is (and that doesn't mean it isn't going to change).

Remember, ACES describes a *co-creative process*. It doesn't end. It spirals onwards, and upwards. What you are given in each moment is the next gift you are invited to respond to and work with. Some gifts come in the form of great successes and are to be celebrated. Some come in the form of challenges to be faced. Both scenarios are to be welcomed—because we really have no other choice. What is, is. The question then becomes: do we embrace what is, or resist it? Are we in or out of synch with it? One way is stressful, jarring. The other is harmonious, fluid, flowing.

Gratitude for each type of outcome puts us in the most powerful and empowered position for our next step. Whether we initially celebrate or feel sorrow, we begin again—cycling back to the Awareness part of ACES, and the next step on life's beautiful journey.

This is the value of Surrender. Not the lie-down-and-submit, hands-in-the-air, "I give up!" kind of surrender. No. The open-minded, open-hearted, "ah... so *this* is what's given to me to learn from next" kind of surrender. The riding-the-crest-of-a-wave kind of surrender. The kind of surrender that dances with its best friends, acceptance and gratitude.

The kind of surrender that invites *you* to join the dance too.

What dance? The dance of life-in-this-moment. The dance of creation-in-motion.

The dance that you ultimately *are*.

It ends, as it began—in Awareness. And the cycle begins again...

VIII. CONCLUSION AND NEXT STEPS

I learned early in life that we carry within us innate wisdom that guides and supports us through thick and through thin. It never leaves us. (How could it? It's what we're made of.)

There are many words for it. Some call it Spirit. Some call it Tao. Some call it the Field. Some call it the Universe. Some call it God. Some call it the Ground of Being. Some call it Divine Energy. Some call it the Infinite. Some call it Life with a capital L.

(It doesn't really matter what we call it. If I have to call it anything, I usually call it Love.)

What matters is that we remember that we *are* it. The ACES Methodology helps us to remember that—and to find our unique expression of it. I call that unique expression our *soulful creative blueprint*. Soulful, because it emanates from our very core; creative, because it is what wants to be expressed and brought into this world through us; and blueprint—because it's there, waiting patiently, utterly immovable, just ready to be discovered, unfolded, and built upon.

To fulfill my own soulful creative blueprint, I help other people to discover theirs. I do this in my books, including **How to Find Your**

Vital Vocation: A Practical Guide to Discovering Your Career Purpose and Getting a Job You Love; in my trainings, including ***Tarot to the Nines*** and ***Tarot Coach Session Success;*** and in my consulting work and coaching packages, including ***Insight Coaching for Soulful Creatives.***

If you'd be interested in exploring how we might work together, here's where to find me:

Instagram:
https://www.instagram.com/briancormackcarr
Facebook:
https://www.facebook.com/cormackcarr
Facebook group:
https://www.facebook.com/groups/tarottothenines
Website:
https://www.cormackcarr.com

ABOUT THE AUTHOR
BRIAN CORMACK CARR

Brian is a certified coach, an Amazon bestselling author, and chief executive of *BVSC The Centre for Voluntary Action,* a leading UK-based charity which supports local community activism and positive social change. His mission in life is helping soulful creative people to connect with their true nature so they can find their gifts and talents and use them to turn their long-cherished dreams into a reality. A long-time student of the world's mystical traditions and the tarot, Brian has combined the modalities of coaching and divination in his bespoke *ACES Methodology,* a powerful coaching framework which blends mindfulness-based nondual awareness practice with cutting-edge goal-setting processes and motivational techniques. He supports his clients through his books, including: *How to Find Your Vital Vocation: A Practical Guide to Discovering Your Career Purpose and Getting a Job You Love* and *Real Food Revival Plan: How to Eat Well, Get Fit and Lose Weight – on the Delicious Diet You Design;* his courses, including *Tarot Coach Session Success* and *Tarot to the Nines;* and his coaching packages, including *Insight Coaching for Soulful Creatives.* Brian is a passionate advocate of charitable activity and community social work. He is a former chair of *Birmingham Race Action Partnership* and *Healthwatch Birmingham* and is currently Senior Independent Director of *Trident Social Housing Association* and a board member of *Birmingham Children's Trust.* He lives in Bournville, England with his partner of 24 years and their little black cat.

Instagram:
https://www.instagram.com/briancormackcarr
Facebook:
https://www.facebook.com/cormackcarr
Facebook community:
https://www.facebook.com/groups/tarottothenines
Website:
https://www.cormackcarr.com

2

BRIAN MATZKE

BROKEN OPEN: A SPIRITUAL AWAKENING & JOURNEY THROUGH PTSD

A Prayer For Living
Life break in me whatever needs to be broken.
Fix my hope of ever being fixed.
Use me, draw every ounce of creativity out of me.
Help me live a radically unique life forever forging a never before trodden path in the forest.
Show me how to love more deeply than ever thought possible.
Whatever I am still turning away from keep shoving in my face.
Whatever I am still at war with help me soften towards, relax into and fully embrace.
Where my heart is still closed show me the way to open it
without violence.
Where I am still holding on, help me to let go.
Give me challenges and struggles and seemingly insurmountable obstacles if that will bring an even
deeper humility and trust in the intelligence of life. Help me laugh at my own seriousness.
Allow me to find the humor in dark places.
Show me a profound sense of rest in the midst of the storm.

Don't spare me from the truth ever! Let gratitude be my guide.
Let forgiveness be my mantra.
Let this moment be a constant companion.
Let me see your face in every face.
Let me feel your warm presence in my own presence. Hold me when I stumble.
Breathe me when I can not breathe.
Let me die living, not live dying.

The shaman says when you find yourself sick you must ask these three questions ...

When did I stop dancing? When did I stop singing? When did I stop listening to stories?

Brothers and Sisters, now is the time to listen to my story and my hope for you is that in my journey of sharing my pains and sufferings a light will shine on your own pain and suffering illuminating them to your greatness.

I lay awake at night wondering if I'm dying, my heart races and panic fills my body. Pain emanates from my organs. I feel like I'm going crazy. Am I losing my mind? Am I dying? If I could be through all this and be healthy again or even be functional in the world without dizzy spells or panic attacks, this I pray for continually.

I am a living breathing example of walking through the fire and I'm here to tell you that life after the death of a career, a body, and an identity is possible. PTSD doesn't have to be forever; you can heal your body and your mind. The traumas that your body holds will give you the messages you need to transform the pain into purpose and step down the road farther into healing and enlightenment..

The medicine is all around you, all you need to do is listen to your body and dedicate yourself to healing.

When we are no longer able to change a situation we are challenged to change ourselves

~Victor E. Frankl

ACT 1- MAN OF THE HOUSE

Born at home in the French quarter of New Orleans to a father who was an artist, musician, and addict. To a mother who loved my father dearly and who wanted nothing but the best for her baby boy.

Early in the morning of January 2, 1979, with the help of two midwives, I made my way into this world under a golden lit room as my father and sisters welcomed me. I stepped into this world in a gathering of love and adoration.

Being a son with a father came to an end very abruptly. At the tender age of two and a half, my father left and was to never return. We found later he had taken his motorcycle for a ride into the country and had a stroke but this news and his body were not found until over a year later.

I carried this grief my whole life and being that I was not young enough to communicate my feelings they got stuck in me. This relationship with the inability to speak my emotions riddled me my entire life and I saw it play out throughout my relationships and my careers. I learned many years down the road that unexpressed emotions no matter what they are tend to simmer inside as the emotion of anger.

My days as a care free child seemed to come to an end at the age of seven years old. This was when I began working at a local grocery store bagging groceries and stocking shelves. What didn't come into my awareness until my late 30's was that when my father died I felt abandoned and unsafe. In order to create that safety, I had to start taking care of myself. Working gave me money to buy the things I needed and a false belief in safety. The wild thing was it wasn't until thirty-plus years later I heard an old man telling a story of working as a child and being able to buy anything he wanted as two young children around the age of seven were near me that a bell went off. I saw these young kids and thought what the fuck was I doing working at such a young age?! Their innocence and tenderness hit me hard and I cried tears of sorrow for my younger self to carry that weight he carried.

As I grew older I searched for systems to help me feel safe and I found that in sports. Sports gave rules and structures and an outlet for my emotions. The old paradigm of guys don't cry except during sports and birth is a place that felt safe to me. I came to find out that even though I was in these highly masculine environments I felt like an outsider most of the time because deep down inside I felt everything so intensely and there was a sensitive feminine side that needed and wanted to be expressed.

A young man without a father creates deep wounds inside and constant searching for acknowledgment and self-worth. Sports gave me this medicine I was seeking but this was an external acknowledgment and worthiness. It took a long time before I truly felt this teaching in my soul and found my inner authority and self-worth.

My mother loved me dearly but bless her heart because she didn't know how to communicate her emotions especially after my father died. So I didn't have an example to show me how to be soft and express my inner emotions. The emotions she expressed were usually control or anger. These both I recognize now as a coping mechanism for the fear and grief she carried. To keep me safe she controlled all aspects of my life. This mirrored my romantic relationships as an adult. I found many people to love me but as soon as I began to let them in my wounds of control and manipulation came out and I would head for the door. I also came to learn that through the wound I carried abandonment whenever a woman began to get too close to me. I would push them away to ensure that my inner child didn't feel the wound of abandonment again.

My mother blessed me with her love of meditation by introducing me to Siddha Yoga at the age of seven years old. I would join her regularly for Satsang and Meditation. I loved going to the gatherings ,chanting and falling asleep as Guru Mayi gave her beautiful teachings. I know now as a Clinical Hypnotherapist how impressionable the subconscious mind is and feel so lucky to have mine filled with love and deep spiritual teachings during these meditations as a child. I was blessed to go to upstate New York one summer with my mother to the Siddha yoga ashram and receive the blessing of Shakti Pat from Guru Mayi. This is a very special blessing that plants the seed for the Kundalini energy to be awakened when the practitioner is ready. I didn't know how impactful this seed was that had been planted until many years later when it flowered.

People will forget what you said

People will forget what you did

But people will never forget

how you made them feel

~ Maya Angelo

ACT 2- SUPERMAN

25 years old, young and fit, and a need for excitement. Well, this led me to the fire department. I had been a college football player and

studied health. I worked in different areas of hospitals from Psychiatric Ward to Labor & Delivery so this brought it all together.

It was November 2004, my head was shaved and I was standing at attention with 30 other fire cadets while getting yelled at as the snow came down on our freshly shined boots. Day after day we did pushups and squats and ran sandhills. I loved it! We were getting paid to do exercise, man it couldn't get any better. 16 weeks later we hit the concrete as new probationary firefighters and in the field known as "fuckin rookies". I'd hear guys say " man I got more time on the shitter than you have on the job". This was true. I was fresh-faced and excited for the next call. It didn't take that long until I got my first fire. I was working at Engine 15 and we got a call about the smell of smoke. We walked through the house checking for smoke, there were no signs really of anything. When we got to the back door we saw black smoke pouring out of the second-story window. The other firefighter and I ran back to the truck to grab the line "fire hose" and stretch it up to the apartment on fire. When we went to the second story you couldn't see anything. It was pitch black. We started making our way down the hallway and checking all the rooms on the way for anyone who was trapped. When we made it to the back room the bedroom was on fire so we began to extinguish the flames, as the flames died down I heard the other firefighter say we have a victim in the bathroom. I dropped the hose and began to help him carry the victim down the hallway. I had a good grip on the guy's arms but the skin was burned so eventually, it let loose like a long pair of gloves and we had to stop. I repositioned my grip and we continued down the stairs outside to fresh air. Paramedics began CPR immediately to no avail and I would place the first of many deaths into a compartment in my mind and body that would one day overfill.

Living in the fire house is like being in a football locker room for 48 hours. The environment is mainly male-dominated with big egos and big hearts. Our nervous systems were on constant alert no matter if we were on a call or sleeping or just sitting on the couch. Because of this environment for our minds and bodies, we often played pranks on each other. The regular prank most young firemen went to were fireworks. We would throw them down the hallway or in the shower or the toilet. Big kids with big toys are what we called ourselves. One station I was at for a long time was station 13 and our emblem was the joker so you can only guess how many pranks filled our sleepless days and nights. We had a tradition of cooking spam and eggs at 4 am if we got calls at that time. Let me tell you we ate a lot of 4 am spam and eggs!

Growing up as a kid that had lost his father I took on the savior role for my mother and sisters. This made sense when I became an adult I'd pick a career where I could be a real-life superman. This was never as true as when my career path in the fire department led me to the Squad two assignment. I had been on the job for about 10 years and had seen more trauma and death than anyone should in their life. I picked this truck because it had the most high-level training in heavy extrication, rope rescue, swift water rescue and structural collapse rescue. We were the guys known as the super squad. My ego and savior complex was thoroughly satiated. This super assignment came with its super weight of trauma. The emergency calls got more severe and my body and mind started to run out of compartments to store it all.

Life as a firefighter takes its toll little by little over time. We worked 48-hour shifts with 4 days off in between. I didn't know that my nervous system was taking a beating year after year and my psyche was also taking its share of horrific memories. When I look back I wish that just as we were required to take tests in the academy and fill out our probationary skills book that we would have been required to receive some sort of therapy. It took me 14 years on the job in the field before it wasn't a choice anymore but an emergency called in by my own body and mind to receive help.

Yoga found me again just after a few years into my career as a firefighter. I feel so blessed to have this counter balance to my lifestyle of sleep deprivation and full-throttle fight or flight nervous system. I feel like I met a double-edged sword when I found yoga again because it was hot yoga that got me hooked. 130-degree classes for 90 minutes and I was doing them sometimes twice a day! A nervous system that is mainly in fight or flight seeks that out in its every day activities. I didn't know this then but I am keenly aware of it now. Most firefighters seek out adrenaline-pushing activities to keep that high that the body is in while running emergency calls. I found this to be true in my every day life, I found this to be true in my everyday life, Extreme hot yoga, Crossfit, Alcohol , Sex. I found a way to find my high I got on the job in many other endeavors in my life.

14 years of living a life of on or off, full go or not at all, fight or flight or total exhaustion I opted to get out of the field and go to paramedic school. This meant eight hour days for six months of high-level schooling on how to be a field doctor i.e. paramedic firefighter. I enjoyed being in the learning environment again and even more so I enjoyed being out of the field of sleepless nights and seeing traumas. I was 4 months into the program when my body began to emit its message to me. I was starting to get anxiety and panic attacks. My stomach and digestion were terribly off. I felt taken by surprise by all of these symptoms. Little did I know that this is something that firefighters often go through especially as they take on a regular schedule or working days and sleeping nights. My body had been used to shift work for 14 years and this total reversal was throwing me off. I decided to go to counseling and see what was going on in my body and mind. This was a bucket of worms I wasn't ready to open yet.

We've got to live, no matter how many skies have fallen."

-- D. H. Lawrence

ACT 3- BROKEN-INNER ALCHEMY

The Serpent Awakens

The body reacts profoundly in trauma. It tenses in readiness, braces in fear, and collapses in helpless terror. When the mind's protective reaction to overwhelm returns to normal, the body's response is also meant to normalize the event. When this restorative process is thwarted, the effects of trauma become fixated and the person becomes traumatized- Waking The Tiger Healing Trauma- Peter A. Levine

I began to uncover my traumas in therapy little by little. My body was screaming at me now and I was forced to listen. I received a diagnosis of Post Traumatic Stress Disorder (PTSD) and was starting to become fully aware of my childhood wounds and how my time as a firefighter had scarred me. Trauma can look very different for many people and surface at any time. The body holds the memory of so many things and because the senses are linked to our subconscious mind just a smell or taste or feeling can bring us back to the traumatic event. This is oh so frequent an occurrence for firefighters. We smell something and it takes our mind and body right back to the horrible scene of the accident.

My body was now in full trauma healing crisis mode. I had left paramedic school and was struggling to get through each day. My body shook and vibrated almost continually. I woke up often tearing my bedroom apart in horrible nightmares. I went through long bouts of insomnia and when my body was almost asleep it would startle itself awake. I was in this weird place where my body was so tired and just ready to sleep but my nervous system was still on high alert and wouldn't let me. My emotions riddled me through intense anger and sorrows. Pain shot all throughout different areas of my body. I often just cried for hours and thought of suicide to help it all stop.

My body felt broken and I was losing all hope that I could ever function in the world. I came into very clear awareness that I could not go back to the career I once loved. This was such a hard realization because in some ways I felt I had no choice and that with a mind and body that we're incapable of doing what once came so easy to me. I had always been the strongest and the fastest and now I could barely walk around my house or drive to the grocery with out having a panic attack. Life felt not worth living anymore.

The longer I stayed away from my old career as a firefighter the more I began to understand the toll it had on me emotionally, physically, psychologically, and spiritually. I was starting to understand that even if my body healed I consciously couldn't go back to that way of living. I was killing myself in many ways.

It took time for me to understand that I was not only healing from a life of trauma and fight or flight but I was also grieving the loss of a career, a family, and an identity. I began to understand the weight that being a firefighter held in my consciousness. The self-worth and confidence that I searched for as a child without a father had been fulfilled through being this super hero of a man. My identity fell away farther and farther from who I was as a firefighter. I realized I was changing from the inside out and this began to reflect in my relationships and what was becoming important to me.

After yoga found me again it wasn't long till I was called to become a teacher. This path felt like yin to my yang of being a firefighter. It was as if I had two lives and two selves. The more in-depth I got into the practices and philosophies, the world of the fire house locker room life felt so dynamically opposed. I saw life differently and I saw people differently. It wasn't until I left the fire department and my body began to release all it was carrying that the energetic and subtle teaching of yoga awakened in me.

As the weight of the traumas I carried slipped away my sensitivity to the world and its energies awakened. I began to feel everything and it seemed that I was a sponge for emotions. This became immensely challenging to go anywhere. The vibrating that I had felt all through my body became more aligned with the central channel of my body.

My thoughts felt uncontrollable at times and it took grounding myself by walking on the earth barefooted to pull the energy back down that seemed so chaotic in my head. I thought I was going crazy before all this happened, now I was almost sure of it. I started to study more the nuances of the energy of Kundalini and how it awakens in the body. This occurrence can not be that different from the symptoms of PTSD, so I believe for myself there was not this and then that. I believe it was all happening simultaneously. The horrible pains I experienced in my sacrum were not just traumas being released, this was the opening of my first energy center to allow this energy to flow. The dizziness that I felt was not only my brain healing from all the traumas and sleep deprivation, this was also my higher energy center awakening. The energy of Kundalini Shakti sits at the base of the spine like a coiled serpent and when it rises it spirals up the spine to the top of the head. When this energy awakens it becomes very challenging but it can also be smooth and beautiful. Each person's journey of this energetic expression is different but what it creates is an explosion of expression and creativity which is the essence of life. This is also dangerous energy and when rushed can cause psychosis. So it's a very slippery slope to rush this energy awakening. The story of Adam and Eve is the story of the kundalini energy. The snake is the energy and the forbidden fruit is the fruit of kundalini knowledge. When this energy is awakened before its time it can be disastrous but when nurtured In its own divine timing it births a beautiful awakening.

I believe that all that has happened for us is creating the current person who we are now and paving the way for who we are becoming. 14 years of being a firefighter and pushing my body and mind to the limit all while simultaneously practicing and studying yoga and meditation were the perfect equation to powerfully open me up to a new way of being in the world. The seed that was planted by Shakti Pat when I was seven years old was now beginning to flower.

As you start to walk out on the way the way appears

~Rumi

ACT 4- MEDICINE AS SELF CARE

I now decided to officially leave the fire department and embark on healing myself. In some ways, I wasn't sure of my decision because there was so much uncertainty in it all. Would I ever be strong enough mentally and physically to live a normal life? I didn't know but what I did know was that the life of emergency calls at 3 am and a nervous system that was in continual fight or flight was not for me any more. So I took the chance and said yes to my mental, physical, and spiritual well-being.

I began with what I knew, Yoga. My internal organs hurt so often and I was dizzy most days that I had to do yoga that was indicative and restorative to my symptoms. So first I went to the sister science of yoga called Ayurveda. This is scientific teaching based on yogic philosophy that spans over 5,000 years old. I used these methods to help the anxiety I felt. I began to eat on a universal body clock to heal my digestion and to begin to normalize my circadian rhythms. I used very specific breathwork practices to heal my hormones that had gone way out of whack from all the stress and sleep deprivation. Multiple times a day I practiced Yoga Nidra which is a very exact science of body meditation that takes you through all the parts of the body to exhibit a deep state of relaxation, one hour of this practice was equivalent to four hours of sleep. I knew if I wasn't sleeping at night I could help the body access these same states in other ways and begin to heal. I was to face my healing the way I did everything else in my life with full enthusiasm and effort.

During this time I came across a group that met weekly that offered EFT- Emotional Freedom Technique/Tapping and Acudetox. EFT is a technique in which you tap certain acupuncture points and say affirmations to help the body release what it was holding. Acudetox is an auricular acupuncture technique used for Trauma and addictions. In fact, this method was brought to the states and promoted by the black panthers to help communities dealing with addictions. These methods helped me dynamically and heavy amounts of trauma began to heal and slough off of my body.

I no longer had a job per se that I had to report to weekly instead my new assignment was my self- healing and this was a full-time gig. I got connected with an Equine therapy program that offered services to Military Veterans and since I was one myself I qualified for their programs helping vets with mental health healing. Now let me tell you when I found this program it was a god send because as a child I did some horse riding and had a special connection with them. I got to meet this big beautiful black horse named Watson. He was very special and had many similarities to me. He was not only big , powerful, and muscular he was traumatized and had anxiety issues. He was a mirror to who I was and what I was going through in my life. This was also the beginning of a beautiful relationship with horse medicine that I now offer to help people and horses heal.

There was this inner energy that pushed me to find as many healing modalities that it would take to get well again. I learned Qi Gong and it was a very needed ingredient to this roux. I was mixing up inner alchemy. Most illnesses come from a deficiency of Qi or Life force energy in the body. Qi Gong helped me build this life force up again from the inside out. Many people these days are pushing the limits of exercise and fitness but what they don't know is most of these activities deplete the Qi energy of the body. So I used this new found method and in doing so my strength built up again little by little.

I next found Craniosacral Therapy and this was an even deeper step into the healing of my nervous system and releasing trauma. The basis of this specific style of craniosacral work was to come into a place of deep relaxation and in this space, the body begins to heal.

I was beginning to truly heal but it didn't seem fast enough and many days I still felt helpless and hopeless. I realized I was carrying inner anger towards my broken body and perceived Illness. I say perceived because all illness is just a message from the body that has been trying to get to us for a long time and when it manifests as a full-blown pathology it is then screaming its message at us. No matter how much I wanted to heal I had to surrender over and over to divine timing and let the process happen. This perhaps was the hardest part of it all.

Trevor Hall says it best-

> You can't rush your healing
> Darkness has its teachings
> Love is never leaving
> You can't rush your healing
> Your healing
> You Can't Rush Your Healing
> -Song by Trevor Hall

I came to the clarity that as I was healing and changing so too was my life and identity. This birthed the perfect time for Hypnotherapy to step into my awareness. In some ways I thought it was something I hadn't experienced before but I was mistaken. I had been practicing deep states of hypnosis just like meditation and yoga Nidra for a long time, so this therapy was very familiar to me. I used Hypnosis to practice more and more conscious relaxation and affirmations. I realized how many of my subconscious beliefs were created. I now understood mass hypnosis of our culture and current belief structures.

I changed my behaviors little by little to encourage new neural-pathways to develop for the person I now wanted to create. I entered my house from a different door, I changed the way I parked my car. You may wonder how these simple things can change who you are, well they make a big impact. Our habits are ingrained into our neuro pathways and they act as a highway we are driving down each day of our life often unconsciously. I knew I had to change the road map of my mind if I was to heal and become someone different.

Our cells take 90 days to die and be reborn so the process of unfolding into a new self takes time but with conscious choice and actions we can steer ourselves into the direction we choose and our body and mind will support us. Change happens progressively and our habits create who we are becoming not today but down the road.

I knew that the process was going to take even more work than I perceived but in the end, it was creating a self and a life I wanted to live.

>Sometimes you have to play a long time to play like yourself
>
>-Miles Davis

ACT 5- FAITH

My path of healing and absorbing wellness modalities lead me to open a private practice as a Clinical Hypnotherapist and Craniosacral Therapist. I also offered private Yoga, Qigong, and Mindfulness to Veterans. My self-worth skyrocketed again and I fully became aware of what my time and life experience were worth. It became very clear to me that I could make a good living on this path and many days as I sat in a deep trance with my clients I felt so blessed and fulfilled that my days were filled with peace and wellness. Through all the healing I had done I learned that my self-care would now take priority. I now created my schedule seeing four to five clients a day and working three days a week. This was a big step from the life I lived as a firefighter. Underneath it all, I was still trying to save people, and many days I still walked away exhausted energetically from absorbing other people's pains and suffering.

This path I was on was paving the way or so I thought to going to graduate school to become a doctor of Chinese medicine. I had the affirmation plastered in my house, "I receive 100,000 dollars or more for acupuncture school.I read it multiple times a day and couldn't step anywhere in my house with out seeing this statement, I believed it and knew it would happen. One year into having my private practice my dream was to become a reality. I got the amazing news that I had been granted $100k for my schooling to become a Doctor of Chinese medicine, I was elated. I remember sitting in my car after I left the office receiving the news and I just cried. I knew my soul path was in alignment and I felt so supported.

It wasn't long before the school semester was about to begin, I received all my books and the curriculum of requirements to be completed in my four year program. One thing I remember all along during the time leading up to the start date of school is I had this feeling that I still wasn't sure this was my soul's path. I loved Chinese medicine and had been studying it for the two years leading up to school starting and felt like I couldn't get enough. I had become a Tao hands practitioner and was studying the teachings of the Tao. I began to use the energy of the Tao to help people heal and through understanding its power and the deep rooting in Chinese Medicine I felt even more aligned with my soul's purpose.

School preparation was beginning and I browsed through the curriculum. I all of a sudden felt this intense constriction of who I was becoming. I saw the box of the learning environment and I disagreed with it, I saw the requirements of the state and acupuncture board and saw myself being limited. I then understood that becoming a Doctor of Chinese medicine was my inner child seeking its self-worth and approval again. I was searching for another career to play the superman role " Doctor". I thought " But the universe aligned me to receive a fully paid education, doesn't this mean this is my path? A dear friend once told me " you can be a great manifestor but it doesn't mean it's for you" Well this was becoming true! Since my departure from the fire department, I have become a

Clinical Hypnotherapist, a Craniosacral therapist, an Acudetox specialist, and Qi Gong teacher. I studied Chinese Medicine, Horse Medicine, Trauma, Grief, and Renewal. I had a plethora of my own experiences of healing. Now was 4 years of school to just add more credentials and pad my self-worth?

I felt afraid to make this choice but in my heart, it felt right, so I walked. $100k given to me, a master's program to become a doctor was I crazy!? My heart felt at peace.

It is very important to understand that our hearts and souls know the way. When we are in the womb our heart is the first thing that is developed and in it are 40,000 brain cells, This is our first brain. If we listen to this brain we will align ourselves with our true nature and path.

Music is Life Itself

~Louis Armstrong

ACT 6- THE JUMP

The pandemic began and I shut down my private practice. My days were very much like ground hog day. My enjoyments came from walking in nature, playing capoeira, and finding simple pleasures. Life was changing all around me and I was being called to the ocean,

So I bought a ticket and made my way down to Mexico. Something happened when I was flying over the mountains on our descent in to the airport. I saw the beautiful lush green and the mist over the mountains and something felt familiar and my heart opened, I began to cry.

Mexico opened my heart more and more each day and a sense of play came out in me. For the first time in my life work wasn't the priority but play was taking precedence. I spent long days in the jungle talking to no one and in silence. I walked barefoot on the soft mud of the jungle paths, I began to learn to surf, I played capoeira regularly. I gave myself permission to have fun. I started teaching conscious connection with horses. I began working with clients again in a magical jungle setting. I felt my path opening up just as my heart. When I was on the edge of making my decision to walk away from school I felt like I had 2 choices. One path led me down a structured road of education and all the beliefs that come with that societal structure, the other path led me to Mexico and a wide-open opportunity and a total unknown. This is where many of us get stuck and we often choose the known route. For what feels like the first time in my life I was choosing the unknown.

Here is what I can tell you now as I've made Mexico my home. The universe is expansive and unlimited so are our options. In our linear way of thinking, we often think we have to choose this or that, But this is not true. All things are possible and just because we can't see it right now doesn't mean it's not possible. My world back in the US had become a place of comfort and safety. My fears were safe inside me and I was able to tailor my life in a way that kept me in that box, my higher self had bigger plans. My new life opened opportunities I hadn't even conceived. My deep wounds of self-worth and confidence fully came to the surface. My fears of death showed themselves over and over again. My nervous system was triggered again and again until it began to normalize. All the places I had been hiding from myself or stuffing down came to the surface.

I'm here to tell you that healing is not linear and nor are your choices and options for your greatness. As we begin to say yes to our self-nurturing and face the wounds we carry, the world opens up in a whole new way. There will be many days it feels as if we can't get from under our own shadow but if you move your body the shadow will move too. Our breath holds a special key to releasing many aspects of our shadow that carry the emotions that hold us in a state of struggle. If we just connect to our breath and use it as a vehicle to move our emotions our perception of the world will change. Line your toolbox with as many healing modalities as you can so that what ever job needs to be done you will have the proper tools. This is what I know, when we don't know where to go next or how we can heal just ask for help and it will show up. Trust that often it won't show up in the way you think but if you are open and listen it will be the perfect way for you. We have all the answers we need inside. We must make a conscious choice to create the time and space to listen. We must have the courage to be different and be uncomfortable. This is part of the beautiful medicine that not only we need but the world needs too. Society will try to keep you stuck in a career, a relationship, and an identity, but when you truly understand that your purpose here is to be a unique signature of you, only then will the world truly open.

This existence is called the divine play of consciousness, We have come here to play. Remember what you loved as a child and seek that out. Take yourself and the world less seriously. Laugh more, smile more, and play more and in doing so you too will find the secret of life my friends.

This book shares the stories of many amazing men that are awakening to their purposes and hearts. May these stories be a light in your path to awaken to your sacred masculine rising and walk with us. A light that shines in darkness illuminates for all to see. Be the light my friends.

ABOUT THE AUTHOR
BRIAN MATZKE

Brian Matzke is a former Firefighter and US Navy Veteran. He is the creator of The Breath of Life Method a full spectrum practice of Qi Gong, Meditation & Somatic Breathwork. Brian is a true horse whisperer and teacher of conscious connection with horses. Being a Craniosacral Practitioner and Clinical Hypnotherapist he is a master of deep meditation and trance. Brian thrives on teaching and sharing his gifts with others. He is currently based in San Francisco, Nayarit, Mexico offering multiple modalities and retreats to people that are ready to heal and transform.

Website: Lightempowered.com
Instagram: light_empowered
Link Tree: https://linktr.ee/Light_Empowered

3

DANIEL T. EDWARDS

ESCAPE THE RAT RACE & LIVE LIFE ON YOUR TERMS NOW!

The sun is shinin' & the weather is sweet in the streets of *Half-Way-Tree*, Kingston, Jamaica. The energy is a frenetic hive of activity as people hustle & bustle through their daily assignments like diligent teacher's pets. In the midst of the organized chaos, a strange, slender figure darts in & out of the throng like a tailor's needle. His eyes cut every direction frantically, beads of cold sweat bedazzle his furrowed brow & his breathing is frenzied, heaving to & fro like a fishing boat trapped in a thunderstorm. The look on his face screams inexplicable terror as he desperately tries to hide behind signposts, dumpsters, walls & barricades as he hurriedly navigates this mini-metropolis in peak-hour traffic.

To his amazement, no one notices as he makes one last run for it across Half-Way-Tree Road with his manhood cupped in his right palm & his ass crack in his left. Not even the woman standing directly in front of him whose eyes are locked with *his* raises as much as an eyebrow or even bats an eyelid as he scurries along. "How come they don't realize I'm naked?" he screams internally, then suddenly a deafeningly jarring noise starts permeating the air urgently & aggressively. BRRRRR-BRRRRRR-BRRRRR

It's 6 a.m. & my alarm is blaring- I am terrified, my bed is SOAKED in my sweat & I am hyperventilating. I frantically pat myself down, realize

I'm fully clothed & breathe a DEEP sigh of relief. "ahh it was all a dream"

I mumble to myself. This is my fifth time now having this same, exact nightmare & it won't be the last. I used to watch movies & T.V. shows depicting people having recurring dreams & I would laugh to myself & say "that's impossible". Look at me now, drenched in sweat, tumbling out of bed & stumbling into a new day like a drunken newborn. My work clothes aren't ready, I have no clue what I'm doing today, my fridge is empty & SURPRISE, SURPRISE, I have a flat tyre, the same flat tyre I fixed last week. O.K. the spare is on now but the car won't start & I just remembered what I have to do today- one of those "things" is a sales meeting at work that started over an hour ago. Ugh, I miss the good ol' days. It was all good just six years ago.

It's October 1st,2005 & my first day on contract as a newly minted, bright-eyed, bushy-tailed Life Insurance Salesman for Life of Jamaica. It's Jamaica's largest, most profitable & competitive Insurance company by a mile; a whale in a tropical pond. This was the biggest career opportunity in my life thus far & my personal experience with sales made me overqualified *on paper* to become a huge success.

I began my sales career at the ripe old age of 10 years old in the sixth grade. My mother- the definition of hustle, gave me a large bag of neon green, yellow, orange, & pink friendship bracelets & told me to sell them for two dollars a pop. I questioned her at first because no one else was selling anything at *Mona Preparatory School*, an institution chock full of the progeny of many of Kingston's elite & ambitious aspirants. "I'm teaching you how to generate income on your *own* Daniel" she said & from that moment on a salesman was born. I sold all the bracelets effortlessly, then more shipments came & went. In high school, I sold "Bobbie" & "Tiki" candies from Trinidad

& Tobago. I sold so many Bobbies that I earned the nickname "Bobbie Man". In Community College it was *Pringles, Snickers*, knock-off *Cartier* watches, knock-off *Benetton* & *Gucci* T-shirts. In University it was multi-level, network marketing & now, here I was standing at the gates of the Gladiator school of sales: the life insurance industry, where only the fittest of the fittest survive & thrive. "What makes life insurance sales so tough?" you might ask. Well for five main reasons.

1. Life Insurance is an intangible concept that may or may not deliver what it promises.
2. Nobody wants it. If you need to empty a room just mention that you're an insurance salesman. Tell me how it goes. You're welcome.
3. You are paid STRICTLY commission with no base salary or allowances. Therefore you only eat what you kill.
4. An insurance agent is a corporate athlete whose job is a weekly, monthly, quarterly, semi-annual & annual competition to see who can sell the most policies, earn the most money & retain the most clients. Your worth is based SOLELY on those variables. Your income is public knowledge & you are constantly being compared to & pitted against your co-workers. You literally live life sprinting on a treadmill.
5. If a client lapses his/her policy in the first year in some instances ALL of the commission paid to you previously is clawed back from your salary on the following month or until the arrears are cleared. You literally can earn a *minus* paycheque.

Luckily for me, I loved the business. I was able to write my paycheque, enjoyed the competition, had autonomy & the freedom to work on "my own time" & if I played my cards right, could earn a HUGE bonus.

For the first time in my life, I gave something my ALL.

I was the first one in & the last one out of the office for my first couple of years.

I ate, slept, & shit insurance. I was obsessed, it was all I talked about - much to the annoyance of my loved ones. My hard work was paying off quickly & I was now wearing designer suits to work, Italian leather wingtips, gold cufflinks, won my branch's rookie trophy, hit the top 5 in the company's Rookie of the year competition & qualified for the prestigious, internationally acclaimed **Million Dollar Round Table**. I was also hosting company award ceremonies, taking trips to Egypt, Jordan & Israel, all while juggling a doting girlfriend & a small harem of side chicks on rotation. I copped my dream car at the time too. A black BMW coupe´ sitting low on 18' TSW rims, so low I had to crawl sideways over speed bumps to avoid tearing my front bumper off. I had a bazooka speaker in the trunk, a sunroof, a tan leather interior & kept the windows untinted so people could see me rollin' by with one hand on the steering wheel & my pinky finger pointing to the sky. I was also poised to buy my first piece of real estate with the money I'd been investing in the now popular local investment fund -*OLINT*. I already had a CLEAR vision for the house too. It would have high ceilings, African masks & spears & shields on the walls, & flat-screen tv's everywhere. Not bad for a "yute" from *Mountain Terrace*.

We have a saying in Jamaica- "Chicken merry, hawk deh near" which translates to "when the chicken is merry the hawk is near". All I can say is at that time in my life I was one MERRY fucking chicken.

It's 2008 & I'm in the prime of my successful run as a salesman at Life of Jamaica & just when I thought it couldn't get any better, my boss hit me with the BIG news. "Daniel, normally sales agents have to complete five years in the field before they are eligible to step into management. However, even though you are at the three-year mark I believe you are ready & we want a man like you to run this branch in the future. If you are serious, you can begin management training in a few weeks". Man, I was blown away! "They like me, they really like me!" I gushed & did *the running man* internally while maintaining my cool Scorpionic exterior.

This was my first time really becoming successful at something & also being offered a leadership opportunity. All my life I was neither a follower nor a leader but a lone wolf who abhorred being controlled or dictated to & while charismatic, couldn't be bothered with the tedium of being in charge of other humans. "This is my moment," I thought "it's time to BOSS UP Danny", "Ah your time now," I said while beating my chest like *Usain Bolt* after running **9.58** in the 100-meter dash with "Chariots of Fire" blasting in my head. Pity I didn't know

I was a lamb to the slaughter, completely unaware that the worst three years of my life would begin *now*.

When a life insurance agent is given the opportunity to become a Unit Manager it's only promotion in theory. Your income is only as good as the quantity & quality of the sales agents you are able to recruit & retain in your team i.e., you earn when they earn. I thought that all I had to do was find six hungry salesmen like me & *poof* I'd laugh all the way to the bank. Let's just say that as soon I began the management journey it was glaringly obvious that I was not management material. I had no leadership skills at the time & was more caught up with being a "boss" than a leader. I was unable to successfully attract quality prospects, my personal sales income plummeted as I focused on managing the team. I was losing agents faster than I could recruit them & the whole experience quickly became stressful for me. The stress spiraled into frustration & then rage because I wanted to win so badly. I was morphing into an angry monster who was unable to keep his emotions in check during stressful situations.

I began to snap at clients, my recruits & administrative staff, successfully earning an iron-clad reputation as an anti-social, hotheaded asshole.

The complaints about me came flooding into my manager on a weekly basis. One of my most memorable clashes was with a recruit who I cursed out for coming into the office with his sleeves rolled up & his tie undone. After my F-bomb-infused tirade was over he delivered an ominous message "Daniel, if you don't humble yourself God a go humble yuh!" I scoffed at the moment but his words were eerily prophetic. Now that you're up to speed with the shit-show at my job, let me fill you in on the other exciting news. The BMW-my pride & joy was now breaking down weekly but I refused to sell it because my identity was wrapped up in this money pit on wheels. I thought I needed this car to be SOMEBODY. Things got so bad that the motors for both windows stopped working, the sunroof stopped working, the A.C. stopped working & the car of course wasn't tinted, so now people could watch me cruising through the mean streets of Kingston dressed like a preacher & sweating like one during Sunday service. I had to drive with a towel, open the door at stoplights to let in some air, dry off & repeat. Don't you dare laugh at me! I see you!

Things took a dark turn in the love department too. On my way back from picking up my girlfriend at the airport I decided to stop at the office quickly to get a document I'd forgotten on my desk. While going up in the elevator, I realized I had left my phone in the car. As I looked down from the elevator into my car, I saw my girlfriend busily scrolling through my phone.

Long story short, I went into the elevator in a relationship & exited a single man. Spoiler alert, she's married now & not to me.

Remember the property I was about to buy with the money in *OLINT*? Well, it turned out that *OLINT* was a high-profile Ponzi scheme posing as an investment fund that made its astronomical returns from *forex trading*. If only I had known the age-old investment adage "if the returns are too good to be true, they probably are". The government shut them down & I watched all my hard-earned money & real estate dreams jump headfirst through the window & splatter all over the pavement.

The stress from all these simultaneous crises began to take a toll on my mental, physical & spiritual health. I developed insomnia, began showing early signs of hypertension & now had an enlarged prostate which got me out of bed as much as six times a night to pee. I was learning first-hand that there is a deep connection between stress, negative emotions & dis-ease in the mind, body & spirit. Things began to fall apart when I took a spill in the bathroom & fell directly on my right knee. The pain was excruciating & led to my knee arbitrarily "locking up" at least once a week. I went to see one of Jamaica's leading orthopedic surgeons who informed me that I had a torn meniscus in my right knee, needed to do surgery to repair it ASAP & would be unable to walk for at least two months. My anxiety shot through the roof. "How will I pay for this?", "How will I survive for two months with no income?", "Suppose the surgery isn't successful?" & on & on I spiraled down the rabbit hole of worst-case scenarios, fire & brimstone, fear & self-loathing.

Life began to feel permanently grey. I would toss & turn until three a.m. on a good night & wake up at ten a.m. on a good day. I was a skinny-fat six feet tall, 150 pounds & lived on a Jamaican bachelor diet which read like an instruction manual- "How to get hypertension, diabetes, cancer & a stroke the easy way". I ate stewed chicken & rice, fried chicken & rice, curry chicken & rice, stewed beef & rice, cowfoot & rice and of course brown stewed fish & you guessed it- rice & washed it down with soda or "fruit juice". I bought my dinners from *"Big Taste"*- a popular greasy spoon cookshop, went home & watched the "Daily Show" then "The Colbert Report" every night. The only exercise I got was in my bedroom which was now becoming like an L.A. porno casting couch.

A revolving door of one hollow sexcapade after another. I was emotionally unavailable with a giant icebox where my heart used to be & no amount of *punnany* could melt it.

The date for the dreaded knee surgery had been set & my anxiety continued to escalate as my world continued to look more & more like Britain in the winter. I had never experienced these feelings before. This was more than just "feeling down". I always prided myself in being a "never say die", "can't stop, won't stop" kind of person who "fought to the bitter end" & thought depression was a myth invented by pussies to justify their weakness & lack of determination. As fate would have it, I got a hold of *The Daily Gleaner*, -our oldest newspaper & stumbled upon a depression test. It said, "if you have at least six of these ten symptoms you are suffering from depression". I scored a whopping 9 out of 10. The only box I didn't tick was *suicidal thoughts*. I was floored! "I'm depressed???", "Me???" A wave of shame swept over me & I tucked my tail between my legs & went home.

The next morning, I decided to discuss the issue with my manager & was relieved when he said to me "Daniel, we are in modern times & you don't have to suffer in silence. We have a company Psychologist who offers the first four sessions free of cost." I set my appointment & went to see the man who would become an unwitting participant in writing a major plot twist into the movie of my life.

It was 4:50 pm, I was ten minutes early for my appointment with Dr. Sydney McGill. I was a mixed bag of fear, nervous energy & gleeful anticipation. I had seen a psychologist twice as a child for assessment purposes but this was my first time seeking help on my own & as an adult. In Jamaica, a man seeking any kind of counseling or therapy is frowned upon & seen as a sign of weakness or mental illness. The stigma is real, but at this time in my life, I had zero fucks left to give & wanted my life back.

He looked like an academic, bespectacled Idris Elba minus the muscles. His credentials included Psychologist, Sexologist & Trauma Specialist. He had me complete a depression test & confirmed that I was suffering from mild depression. He then had me complete a Myers-Briggs Personality test—a system that ACCURATELY divides humans into 16 personality types. When he looked at my results he smiled knowingly & released a gentle "ah-hah". "You're an ENTP personality Daniel that's why you're dying on the vine".

"You want to be out & about having fun dynamic experiences every day, not cooped up in an office managing sales agents." Wow! I was blown away! This is literally how I felt every day but my ego kept telling me to keep going.

A so-called promotion that was the dream of many was a nightmare for me. Immediately I thought of the millions of people who got dressed up every day, looking good, smelling good, driving nice cars & were seemingly successful but dying on the inside because their occupations & vocations were misaligned.

He proceeded to ask me a few questions-
Doc- "Do you exercise?" Me- "Only in the bedroom"
Doc- "Do you go back to nature?" Me- "I don't have time for that, plus I'm broke"
Doc- "Do you meditate?" Me- "No, what's that?"
Doc- "Sit, breathe & think of nothing".
Me – "How will sitting & breathing help me get out of this crisis I'm facing?"
Doc- "Daniel, your greatest power will come from your stillness & silence."

He then gave me a five-minute introduction to meditation right there on the spot & I enjoyed it immensely. It felt like I took a mini-vacation from the negativity & self-flagellation tape that was running non-stop inside my cranium.

I intuitively knew at that moment that I had found one of the tools I'd been searching for desperately; a gateway to inner peace.

I left Dr. McGill's office & began what is now a 10-year deep dive into personal development, wellness & transformation. I went to a bookstore across from my company's head office & bought a three-

CD guided meditation box set & set off on my journey like a dog with a bone.

If I had to explain my meditation experience to someone It would sound like this. Imagine looking at a giant wall covered with big screen T.V.s. Each one is on a different channel & maximum volume. Imagine those T.V.s slowly being turned down & turned off one by one until only two or three are left on & sometimes all are turned off. That wall is my mind before, during & after meditation. Taking the time to meditate allowed me to step out of my head & take a bird's eye view of my life. I saw all the scenarios where I was adamant that I was in the right & realized that I was in the wrong. The whole process in some ways was like placing a giant mirror in front of me & I didn't like what I saw.

I knew then that I had to do a *180* with my life. About a week into my new found obsess-oops I mean practice, I started to exhibit bizarre behaviour such as telling co-workers good morning with a genuine smile, holding the elevator open for stragglers trying to get in (instead of letting it close as usual) & here's an even bigger shocker. I had a minor incident in my apartment complex where a neighbour informed me that my bumper had grazed his door while I was parking & rubbed off some of the paint.

I flipped out & cursed him out immediately & went back into my apartment. A few minutes later I went back to my neighbour's apartment, apologized profusely & even offered to pay for the damage. "Who is this guy?" I asked myself "Is this really you Daniel?"

Another interesting episode happened soon after that. One day on my way back from a sale (which I closed) something told me to go back to the beach I went to as a child with my mother every Sunday. It was "Brooks Pen Beach" in the rustic Bull Bay Area just outside of Kingston. The beach was no longer open to the public but the owner still lived there, her name was "Auntie". "Look how yuh grow big," she said & allowed me to enter the beach. I took off my corporate monkey suit, stripped down to my boxers & went swimming on a sunny, empty beach in the middle of a workday. I felt so free! As the Caribbean sea pounded me against the black sand I reconnected with my eight-year-old self: carefree, playful & fearless. I skipped stones off the waves for half an hour just like I used to. I jogged on the sand, played with a one-eyed beach dog & drank in the majestic beauty all around me. Questions started to bombard me in waves. "Why haven't you been to the beach in years? You live in Jamaica." "Why haven't you taken more time for yourself to de-stress & relax?" "Why is insurance & punanny the only thing happening in your life?". From that day forward I began to go back to nature on a weekly basis & haven't kicked the habit & don't ever plan to.

It's December 16th, 2011 & I'm being wheeled into the operating theatre for the dreaded knee surgery. I feel like I am about to face a firing squad. I don't care how minor your surgery might be, once you put on that hospital gown, sit in that wheelchair, lie on that operating table & have an I.V. stuck into your arm, you my friend will come face to face with your mortality & you won't like the feeling. Dr. Phillip Waite was the surgeon. He assured me that the surgery would be a simple forty-five-minute arthroscopic procedure. I was able to watch on screen while he explored the interior of my knee with a tiny camera. Inside of my knee looked like footage from *"Shark Week"* on Discovery Channel after a great white had a feeding frenzy. My meniscus looked all mangled & chewed up. "This is way more serious than we expected Daniel," said Dr.Waite. Six hours later, Dr. Waite had stitched up my meniscus & once the spinal anesthesia wore off, I was free to go home.

The next two months of my life were the darkest, toughest, most painful & transformative period in my life. I literally had nowhere to run or hide physically & mentally for two months. I came face to face with all my transgressions, childhood traumas, demons, fears & failures. I dived deeper & deeper into my meditation practice & the deeper I dived, the more I shed the baggage & junk I had been hoarding internally for decades.

I finally started to realize that I was the writer, producer & director of my life & was the only person responsible for the state of it. It's human nature to blame "them" & what "they did" for our problems but I assure you, if you have a string of problems in your life's equation, take a look at the common variables. If the recurring decimal is *you* then it's YOU, bro. Most of the problems we face within ourselves & the world at large merely require adjustments on our end. Adjust your frequency & the universe will meet you with the same energy. You will find that this approach to problem-solving is far less strenuous as long as you are willing to humble yourself. I now know first-hand that ego is the enemy & a little humility goes a looong way. Humility greases the wheel of life.

Another vital lesson I learned from my ordeal is that the #1 factor in your success equation is the quality & quantity of relationships you're able to attract & maintain. Relationships make the world go round, not money. All my life I was taught "No one gives you anything", "if you want something done well, you have to do it yourself." Or "Trust no one" & the old classic, "Nothing in life is free". This mindset led me to have an adversarial relationship with the world. I was an outsider, a rebel without a cause with a huge chip on my shoulder. When we insist on playing tug-of-war with the world, **EVERYTHING** is difficult. It's impossible to accomplish anything great on *your own*. If you're the world's best singer, good luck feeding your family if no one buys your music or tickets to your shows. The secret to flipping the script on the existing dynamic is approaching life with a value-added mindset. Instead of constantly seeking to reap & extract, think of ways you can maximize the value you contribute to the world. Ask yourself "How can I leave the room better than I found it?".

Of the myriad benefits that meditation furnishes practitioners with, I would have to say my favourite is the fact that it serves as a portal to your Internal Navigation System. The more you explore this frequency, the more you will find yourself intuitively & effortlessly drawn to what serves you & develop an aversion for what doesn't. As an Afro-Caribbean male in a post-colonial, post-slavery society I am very familiar with *drama & trauma*, not *ease & speed*. Meditation has introduced *ease & speed* to my life in novel ways.

My Internal Navigation System began to re-write my life's movie script with many beautiful new additions. I started doing Yoga as a form of rehab for my knee at first & instantly fell in love. Now I practice Yoga daily.

I practice a simple but powerful Tibetan system called the **"Five Rites of Rejuvenation"**. I took my skinny-fat ass into the gym & hit the weights & am now fit & lean at **180lbs**. I may not have a body like *LL Cool J* but I love the skin I'm in. I dropped the toxic bachelor diet & became a pescatarian in 2017 (bye, bye chicken & beef) & while I'm no calorie counter, I definitely have a much healthier relationship with food now. My prostate healed up after my mentor Kevin Wallen introduced me to Paida-Lajin. Google it, you're welcome.

After a deep meditation session, a voice said "sell the stupid BMW & buy something reliable." Well, I sold it & bought a reliable budget car & the world didn't end.

My insomnia slowly cleared up over time & I can once again sleep through a gunfight or a missile launch. I began to attract a conveyor belt of guardian angels into my life in the form of lightworkers & mentors who continue to furnish me with jewels, nuggets & tools to raise my vibration & step into my true purpose.

Speaking of true purpose, there's a "downside" to having a spiritual awakening. Once the veil covering your reality has been lifted you will have trouble operating business as usual. When I returned to work, the first thing I did was step down from management & head back to sales. I enjoyed it at first, went back to my winning ways but the emptiness soon came raging back stronger than ever. "There must be more to life than this Dan. All you do is sell, sell & repeat" I said to myself but would still go blank when the question "what would you do instead?" came up.

It's summer 2016 & I'm receiving a strange request from a friend. "Daniel, I need to upgrade my wardrobe, how do I go about that?" My friend was Rickman Warren, a successful Reggae producer & marketer.

"Umm...I'm an insurance agent, not a stylist Rick" I responded flatly. "Yes Dan, but you're always sharp, help me out," he said. "O.K. fine, I will come by at 7".

It's 7 pm & Rick & I are huddled over his computer like Barack Obama in the situation room the night the Navy SEALs were about to find Bin Laden. In our case, the subject matter didn't involve carnage but was no less strategic. "Are you a lumberjack, what's with all the plaid shirts?" "If you're a marketing guru in the corporate space then Blazers & Sports Coats are your best friend". "Maybe we shouldn't buy ten pairs of the same exact shoe in different colours going forward Rick." Two hours later Rick had bought a new wardrobe online with my help & I went on with my life.

About a month later Rick called back with exciting news "I got the contract; they accepted my proposal!" "I get NON-STOP compliments on my outfits every time I do a presentation, this is awesome!". "All the girls deh pon mi case like Matlock" "Do you know what an image consultant is?" he said. "HAHA NO," I said. "Well, that's a business you could definitely get into. Do all the research you can on how it works". To date, this has been the most bizarre business idea anyone has ever suggested to me & trust me I've heard some BIZARRE ideas. The more I played with the idea, the more ridiculous it seemed & very soon I forgot about it.

It's 8 am, October 2017, YouTube is on autoplay & I hear a very familiar voice giving a motivational speech. It's Steve Harvey- "Your gift will make room for you..." "What is your gift? The thing you do best with the least amount of effort." "Quit running from your gift." At that moment a light bulb went off in my head. "What are my gifts?" I wondered. Sales, public speaking, writing, a great eye for fashion & aesthetics, event planning & execution, an obsession with transformation & an insatiable drive to motivate people. The number *180* kept swimming around in my head for hours & then **BAM! I GOT IT!** I would form a company called **"T180" (as in Total 180)**. Our slogan is *"Nothing Changes if Nothing Changes"* & we're the Caribbean's **FIRST & ONLY** lifestyle brand designed around three pillars- Aspiration, Motivation & Transformation. We operate using six formats: one on one consultation, speaking engagements, workshops, online courses, events & YouTube channel. All designed to help Caribbean people step into their **GREATEST** and **HIGHEST** selves.

The first workshop we created was *"Dress Up & Show* Up" & now we have *"Dollars & Sense"*- a financial literacy course, *"Time is The Master"*- a time management master class, *"Word, Sound & Power"*- a public speaking & oratory course". "The Brand New, Brand *YOU!* Programme"- a comprehensive personal branding master class & *"Move, Breathe...Balance"*- a holistic wellness & transformation programme. Since our launch we have served a number of Jamaica's leading corporate entities, schools and Children's homes.

In 2019 we started *"**Long Story Short...**"* Jamaica's FIRST & ONLY monthly storytelling showcase & live music experience. In 2021 myself & Kevin Wallen & Marlon Birbridge formed the three-man motivational supergroup *"**We 3 Kings**"*. We'll be making some serious impact on the speaker's circuit and Podcasting universe very soon.

Who knew that dabbling in a casual hobby would lead to discovering my true purpose & having the opportunity to help others find theirs too? My role as Chief Visionary Officer of *T180* has thrust me back into leadership again with a team of ten. Though I still have room for improvement, I can say with confidence that I've evolved into a good leader. Here are three of my thoughts on leadership.

1. Being a good leader begins with being a good listener.
2. People don't care how much you know until they know how much you care.
3. True leaders lead from the front and eat last.

It's a bright, sunny Wednesday morning in *Half-Way-Tree*, Kingston, Jamaica. The hive is buzzing as usual & a throbbing Dancehall-driven pulse is the conductor of this colourful & chaotic symphony of cars, Coaster buses, Robot Taxis, Yeng Yeng motorcycles, mission-driven pedestrians & vendors. High above the fray, a strange, slender object is floating between the clouds like a hang glider. On closer inspection, it's actually a man gliding through the sky with his right arm extended like SuperMan. The look on his face says pure bliss with a wide, toothy grin & smiley eyes. He gazes peacefully at the excitement below & gently descends to earth. He is dressed to the nines in a light-blue, linen windowpane suit, a crisp white shirt with gold cufflinks, a pair of mirror-shine two-tone brown wingtips & a navy-blue fedora with a red band in the centre. As he touches down on the sidewalk, he opens his gold pocket watch which says 5 am then suddenly a warm, humming sound starts to slowly permeate the atmosphere, gradually getting louder & louder. GONG-GONNNGG-GONGGGG.

It's 5a.m., my alarm has sounded, I pat myself down & realize I'm naked in bed, laughing to myself I mumble "ah it was all a dream." It's January 1st, 2020 my first day as a **FULL-TIME** creative entrepreneur. Wish me luck.

ABOUT THE AUTHOR
DANIEL T. EDWARDS

Daniel T. Edwards is the Owner & Founder of **T180**: The Caribbean's FIRST & ONLY lifestyle brand designed around three pillars; *aspiration, motivation & transformation*. One which Mr. Edwards created to productively combine his three passions – Personal Development, Wellness & Psychology.

A trained public speaker & presenter, Mr. Edwards launched his series of **T180** Workshops In 2017, the first being through corporate client *Sagicor Life Insurance Jamaica Limited*.

In September of 2018 he took the bold step of launching the Caribbean's FIRST & ONLY Men's lifestyle YouTube channel which has now transitioned into a personal development hub for all.

In September of 2019 he launched **"Long Story Short...Jamaica"**: Jamaica's FIRST & ONLY monthly storytelling showcase/live music experience.

With three decades of successful experience in the sales industry,

Mr. Edwards is a former Senior Sales Executive at Caribbean Assurance Brokers Limited. Prior to this he was a Unit Manager &Financial Advisor at **Sagicor Life Insurance Jamaica** Limited where, among other things, his achievements included being seated at the internationally-acclaimed **Million Dollar Round Table**.

An experienced performer & lover of nature, Mr. Edwards is also a proponent & practitioner of mindfulness techniques, The Wim Hof Method, Paida-Lajin & diverse holistic self-healing practices.

YouTube: T180 Lifestyle & Long Story Short Jamaica

Facebook: T180 Lifestyle & Long Story Short Jamaica

Instagram:

@danieltafareye-instagram

@we3kings- Instagram

@t180lifestyle

4

MATTY RYCE

YOU ARE THE ANSWER

Even though we are all here together on this little blue marble floating in the vast expanse of the universe, every one of us is on our own unique path—looking for truth, for love, for wholeness, for—*something*.

What are you here to discover?

Life—the purpose of it?

The meaning of it all?

I do not have the answers, but what you search for can be found—in you.

I invite you to contemplate your journey, your experiences, your challenges, and your triumphs.

What brings you joy? What evokes fear?

Each and every one of us holds the key to the mysteries locked inside, so look within, and you will find what you are yearning for.

Because at the end of it all, each of us is the hero of our own story.

This is mine.

I grew up as the first-born in a traditional household. My dad, the man of the house, ruled with the proverbial iron fist. Quick to anger but a big heart, he walked an interesting line between stable dependability and erratic sensitivity. Needless to say, this made for a challenge to navigate while growing up. Being "my father's son," this has also been something that I have struggled with on my journey into and through adulthood. Anger is a funny thing. It's been the fuel to many a fire in my life, which in turn, has burned down a number of houses in its wake. As I have learned about astrology, discovering that my moon is in Aries has helped me put some pieces in place with regards to this topic. (A little note on that, in very basic terms: The Moon is said to govern one's emotions, and Aries is the first fire sign of the Zodiac = fiery, passionate emotion). I have come to understand that anger has both the ability to consume and destroy, but also to motivate and propel. I still find myself walking the line between them, although these days, I find myself less involved with "arson" than I used to be. This challenge has presented an opportunity for a lengthy and ongoing evaluation and inquiry into this emotion, its causes, and the results of the ensuing actions. I continue to learn, grow, adapt and evolve.

Despite the perceived irrational outbursts of my dad growing up, I always knew and felt that I was loved and, ultimately, safe. "This is just the way it is" is what I understood. This passion and aggression that I took on, powered my athletic endeavors, which earned me accolades, praise, and fulfillment. The work ethic and perfectionism which I had also seemingly inherited, or perhaps simply came to learn—the ongoing Nature vs. Nurture debate—bled into all aspects of my life. This has been another gift and a curse, as I find myself struggling with this very process as I nitpick every word I write in efforts to produce something of value and substance. Every "t" was to be crossed, and all "i's" dotted; the obsession withof the pursuit of perfection was a driving force, and in many cases, successful. However, one can only juggle so many balls before they start to fall, as I learned in a challenging fashion later on in life when I moved out and all of the responsibility landed solely on my shoulders. Be that as it may, many significant core values, such as love, strength, integrity and humility were imparted on me by my father, and have formed the bedrock from which I have been able to flourish.

My mother, on the other hand, had more of a "shrug and smile" attitude around life. Not without her own convictions as a stubborn Taurus, which resulted in some head-butting with my Capricorn self as I fought to enter adulthood; particularly in that I (debatably) stayed too long in the nest. My mom was the quintessential mother and caregiver; I now look back and am inspired by someone who found their calling and committed so fully to it—from raising her own children to running a daycare for many years. To this day, I speak with Mom for a couple of hours every week, which is a testimony to her driving desire for connection and is something that I have come to both understand and relish—even revere.

It was not always like this.

Feeling the ire for my father at times but being unable to express it towards him, my mother received the brunt of it from me. Being the saint that she is, she was able to receive and transmute it, knowing it wasn't about her. Needless to say, she saved me a lot of confrontations that would not have been to my benefit. But as I moved through adolescence, especially in my early 20's, our relationship had its rocky patches as I was trying to forge my own path while still being under the wing of the home. My mom had her way of doing things and I was trying to impose mine—this was a recipe for disaster that resulted in plenty of bickering between the two of us and a notable chip on my shoulder.

It wasn't until I moved out that the love and appreciation for my mother was wholly felt, and, on her end, there was a recognition and cherishing of the man I was becoming.

Being raised in this balanced, loving household provided me with a great foundation to build on, but true empowering growth comes from facing adversity, and this became more apparent as I ventured into adulthood on my own. Having moved out of a middling, blue-collar city (shout-out to Hamilton, Ontario), I found it challenging to adjust to not only the metropolis of Toronto but also to being fully responsible and accountable for myself. The learning curve for the latter was steep, and I often learned the hard way—I didn't realize how much I had depended on my mom and how much of what she did "behind the scenes" impacted the ease of my life. Sure, by the later years, I was cooking a bit (often by revamping leftovers), but laundry, cleaning, and many of the other household tangibles were foreign to me. Perhaps, but like many people moving out for the first time, this was my initial (and somewhat rude) awakening.

At times, part of me experienced resentment around my pampered upbringing, but I ultimately came to understand this gift and I was grateful to have had the opportunity to focus my efforts on school, sports, and simply being a kid.

Everything worked out the way it is supposed to, and I—or we all, simply don't know what we don't know. I have come to accept this reality, it isn't anyone's fault. We are all just doing our best with what we have.

Acceptance is a crucial part of the process.

Another thing that I came to realize was that the reality I grew up in —an old-fashioned home where Dad ruled the roost and Mom supported in a more submissive manner, was not the reality that I was living in as a "modern man" in a big city.

The litmus test for this could often be found in my relationships with women.

I began to become aware that my mother was a dying, if not nearly extinct, breed of woman. Or perhaps it was that I was living in a wildly diverse cosmopolitan city. Either way, I was intrigued by the independent modern woman, and I spent a lot of time, resources, and energy indulging in this proclivity.

During this period of discovery, I learned a valuable lesson: acting out certain patterns that I absorbed from my father with women who were *not* like my mother, was not going to fly. I repeat—was NOT going to fly.

Spending years on this so-called battlefield during my adult life, I discovered the nuances; I understood how to act and what behaviours were desirable as well as the ones that weren't. My intentions were to be a decent person, a gentleman even, and not to just be some guy simply trying to get laid. However, those lines often became murky, especially with my growing expertise, which was only reinforced by my "success rate."

Be funny, be kind, be respectful, be chivalrous, be charming, be humble (even if perhaps it was more of a false humility at times).

Check, check, check, check, check, check.

Even though they weren't always put to use in the most honourable way, I believe these attributes are of great value. The slippery slope came when the genuine interest in women turned into sport, and I became lost in the pursuit of finding the "perfect" partner to complete me. In a city of 2.5 million people, along with the rising trend of internet-driven instant gratification and the ease of replaceability, there were *many* casualties of this war. These experiences varied from temporary nights, to short-term flings, to on-again-off-again, to living together, and they all taught me a lot about myself, life, what I wanted, and what I didn't. Through these trials, I learned to argue less aggressively, how to compromise, how to be a better partner, and perhaps most importantly—how to be completely content being on my own.

We can only love others to the depth that we can love ourselves.

I travelled solo during several winters to escape the cold, combat Seasonal Affective Disorder, and nurture my soul. Two months in SouthEast Asia in 2018 would prove to be inspiring and life-changing, as well as full of wonder and frustration. As a somewhat cliche right-of-passage kind of adventure for many fresh college graduates, I was 38 and felt the call with an explorative intentionality—both of the land and of self.

It was the concept of intention that had a profound impact on my life, which resulted in a lot of deep introspection and self-enquiry. I came across a quote last year that encapsulated this period for me, it read: "real growth happens when you're tired of your own shit." Whether it was coming home drunk (be it a night out on the town or one of my gigs), or spiralling into a frustrated rage, or feeling useless and unmotivated the "day after" (which often extended beyond that), or unsatisfying dates and unfulfilling relationships (including the one with myself), or lacking general direction and purpose in my life—ALL of this shit was getting old, and I was tired of showing up in this way.

I was in the twilight of my 30's, yes, I've had fun, I have done some awesome stuff (and some dumb shit), I travelled, I chased my younger self's dream to be a DJ, I "loved and lost" (the death of my beloved cat of eleven years was *heavy*), but I was *still* trying to find myself—so, what now?

Asking difficult and honest questions allowed me to look deeper into myself, and I began to consciously make decisions with a heightened awareness. I wasn't drinking to the point of drunkenness, my outbursts had become more sporadic, and I was dating less—even turning down booty calls. Having learned about how we are able to create space for the things we desire, I started to hone that intentionality around what I wanted in my life over what I didn't want. I boosted my supportive daily habits and strengthened my mindset. Another solo trip to the south of Thailand in early 2019 found me at a yoga retreat, deepening my practice, connecting with myself, and revelling in the beauty of this world. However, it would be my return home where I would step onto a new path.

I casually met Audra through a DJ friend during the previous fall at one of my regular gigs. Dark room, loud music, I am always locked into my craft, so it was a simple "Hi, nice to meet you" exchange. We kept in touch over the winter, curious about each other's endeavours —especially with her being a fellow musician; the conversation was friendly with a dash of flirt.

Upon returning from the month away in South Thailand, we decided to finally meet up after chatting for so long. Audra recommended a walk, and despite the difficulties acclimating to the early March weather, I agreed to it—and it was lovely.

Things began very casually between the two of us, and I learned more of her story—leaving an eight-year marriage in Australia to return to Canada and pursue her dream of music. Regardless of the relaxed nature of things, I made the decision to enter into this connection with integrity and intention. I did not want to stand in the way of this woman realizing her dream, and in fact, I honoured it, and her, as much as I could—I even saw her perform on a number of occasions. Audra's journey was inspiring to witness. It also came with its challenges. I had to check my ego many times and uphold my word by making sure my "walk" and my "talk" were in alignment. I discovered how to express myself and my emotions in a respectful and considerate manner. Later I would find out I was using the techniques of nonviolent communication (or NVC for short) without realizing it—no kiddin'!

Even with our casual nature, I continued to choose to show up consistently, with integrity, and remain faithful (which had been a regular challenge in past relationships—casual or otherwise). It felt good, and I felt good, and—strong. I was honouring myself as much as I was her, and because of this, our relationship deepened. I was steadfast and patient; it was beautiful to watch Audra both soften and heal—since her past (like most of us) had left her with some wounds.

We grew together, I helped her work through her trauma, and I found expansion in myself amid this—as if I was being called into something bigger. I performed energy work on her as she healed through her chakras, which gave rise to a Kundalini Awakening in her—like, *Holy shit, I had a hand in that!?* Truth be told, it had its scary moments, but it was fascinating and exhilarating for the most part. Audra now experiences clairaudience and clairvoyance and mentors others with their awakenings. To see how she operates is incredible, and I am honoured to have played a pivotal role in all of this. Who knew that honouring the Feminine by showing up with integrity, consistency, intentionality, compassion, kindness, understanding, and love would lift Her up to this echelon of being.

THIS IS THE WAY.

This is the standard by which I live and teach now.

At the beginning of March 2020, Audra and I travelled to Mexico for some sun, sand, and Ayahuasca. I began hearing the call to the medicine a couple of years earlier but had been patient in my pursuit. That being said, there we were in the vortex of Tulum, about to embark on one hell of a trip. We ventured south of the town to the "retreat" which was essentially a campground, complete with outdoor washroom facilities and a couple of shacks on the beach. But it all felt fine, if not fitting, given the disorganized nature of preceding events. I just trusted and let it flow—this would not have been the case for me several years ago (yay, growth!). Eight of us, plus the facilitator and the Peruvian Shaman, had gathered amongst the palm trees for the ritual. Even though I knew a bit about the medicine and its use, I had little idea what to actually expect. Part of me was filled with excitement, and another part was nervous—I would try to avoid bringing that energy into the ceremony with me.

YOU'RE HERE NOW, JUST TRUST.

Capturing everything that I experienced that night on paper would be a disservice. It was beyond anything I could have imagined, let alone expect. The Oneness was overwhelming; the sand became a tapestry that blended into the trees, everything pulsed in unison with the music. Matter dissolved into its true energetic frequency creating grids of tiny lights. My mind exploded, my senses overloaded, my understanding of reality expanded beyond my comprehension. It was as if The Matrix and Avatar had a baby—this is now my frame of reference. Of course, any proper psychedelic experience comes with its more energetically dense aspects, like seeing dark shadows looming above oneself with a sensation akin to drowning.

Breathe. *Brreeeeeeaaaaaatttthhhhe.*

I questioned whether my breath kept the darkness at bay and propelled me through the journey or if it prevented me from experiencing the darkness. My understanding now is that the breath is our most sacred gift and tool. I witnessed the shadows, and we are able to coexist—the integration of all of that comes later (and continues to be an ongoing practice).

Having respected and given space for our individual experiences, Audra and I came together towards the back end of the journey, and it was beautiful and surreal. Once we returned to our beach shack, our conversation would go on for hours, *and* hours; sleep was neither the focus at this point nor necessary. One of the challenges of the *dieta* was abstinence since sex can mix energies as well as deplete life force, and we wanted to honour the guidelines. But later that night, we connected so deeply, so truly, and with so much desire. There was this realization of this inner masculine, this—Divine Masculine, that was ignited within me; this feeling, this personal empowerment, this fullness.

THIS is who I AM.

Functioning on an hour of sleep and an apple, we entered into our second ceremony—it was just the two of us along with the facilitator, Bernice. Different brew, but the rush of the medicine was the same, that echo-y sensation in my ears as the cold crept in from my arms and over my entire body. The visuals were more fractal-like and linear; the patterns of the blanket blended into my skin and the surroundings of the *palapa*. It was all quite spectacular. I was shown multiple portals, but I was (still) not receiving answers to my questions around clarity of purpose. I lamented aloud while conversing with our facilitator on the beach.

"You can simply do whatever you want to do," Bernice replied.

"Ugghhh, I don't know what I want," I pleaded.

I thought this medicine was supposed to help with this sort of thing.

TRUST. THE. PROCESS.

Earlier, Audra and I had moved to the other available beach shack in search of a breeze that would keep the ravenous mosquitos away, but upon spending the night, we came to discover that this one, in fact, housed a spirit. Yes, that's right, journeying with Aya and spending the night in a haunted beach hut. But I am still here to tell the story, so everything worked out *just fine*.

Night three of this retreat was not so fine for Audra, however, as she experienced what they call "the dark night of the soul". It was once again, just the two of us, under the full moon, celebrating the one year mark since our fateful stroll—what could go wrong? It was ROUGH for my lady, to the point that I pulled myself out from the medicine to help her alongside Bernice. With a lot of care, compassion, and patience, we helped Audra get herself through it, albeit by the skin of her teeth. There were crucial revelations for her though, *and* for me, because, *wait*—I managed to stop the process of the medicine? *Hmmm, interesting*—there might be something in that for me.

We got through the night, back in the original shack after our encounter with the spirit from the night prior. Audra, raw, was left doubting everything she had experienced, and I was feeling a bit deflated and as though things were incomplete. So I did what any normal person would do—schedule a *fourth* night of ceremony—much to Audra's dismay, but she was supportive knowing I didn't get the full experience during that third round.

The setting was special for this one, taking place in a ceremonial tent; there was a little something extra about this night. It was an honour to be doing this one-on-one with Bernice, and it felt like an anointing. I wept as I healed inner child wounds, shook as I received golden life-force, laughed as I found joy, and felt deep humility as I was called into purpose as a healer. The feeling of gratitude was immeasurable.

Thank you, thank you, thank you, from the bottom of my heart.

Returning home with the wind in my sails, I was ready, and guided to find community. Six days later, the infamous lockdown of 2020 began. *Mmmmmhmmmm.*

Towards the end of April, I came across the Tmrw Tday Virtual Festival, the online iteration of a culture and wellness festival that a friend of mine, Andrew Christoforou, put on annually in Jamaica. This was twelve days of workshops of all things wellness—yoga, breathwork, meditation (and *so* much more) with practitioners from across North America, and nightly music acts—all on Zoom. WOW, this was a real life-shifting event. Not only was I able to help integrate the reality-shaking Ayahuasca experience, undergo incredible expansion, but I found this beautiful, loving, and like-minded community.

I'M HOME.

Virtual Fest 2.0 followed shortly thereafter in May due to high demand and rave reviews; everyone felt the importance and magnitude of this work. Another impactful six days, with more expansion, more integration, deepening knowledge, practice, relationships—I even got to contribute by DJing at the "Virtual Disco". Awesome.

Three Virtual Fests, two in-person retreats, and countless events later —I am fully immersed in this flourishing community, involved in the music and workshop facilitation aspects. I am incredibly grateful to have had the stars align the way they did to bring me together with this group of amazing beings. This was one of the big early lessons around trusting the universe—even when it looked bleak after returning from Tulum into lockdown, things worked out better than I could have imagined.

TRUST.
Trust the process.
Trust that you are Divinely supported.
Trust yourself.

My involvement with this community also led me to take part in my first personal development course: The *Future Self Incubator,* with Peter Opperman. This ended up being a remarkable twelve weeks highlighted by shadow work, inspired actions, and creating your ideal life with your highest/future self as the architect. I use the concepts and tools I learned and developed in this program often— both in my personal practice and with clients. We don't refer to Peter as the "wizard" for nothin'.

During this period of acclimation after my awakening experience in Tulum, I joined my first men's group and have been a part of a weekly call with the *Light Warriors Mens' Circle* for over a year and a half. To say that it has been enlightening would be an understatement. It has given me such a depth of understanding of the Divine Masculine— from the complexities of archetypes, to the framework of NVC, to the practices of listening and holding space. My gratitude runs deep for Augie and this powerful container. I am also involved with the Tmrw

Tday community men's gathering: *Menamorphosis*. Being a part of these circles has led me to see the true importance of brotherhood—in my life as well as society, and how it has been lost in the midst of the patriarchal ideal of competition. I realized that despite growing up with a brother whom I was very close to and a father who loved us immensely, having played on countless sports teams, and having many male friends, I was missing this kind of interaction with like-minded men in adulthood. Men who are doing self-work, men who can look you in the eye and *see* you, men who express emotion honestly and mindfully, men who hug you and *mean* it, men who support you and want to see you thrive, men who love you—and who can actually say it, freely, without any hesitation or awkwardness.

This is all a part of the man that I am now, and I fucking love who I am.

I am the *Modern Masculine*, deeply present, aware, and aligned with all aspects of life while embodying a balanced, healthy and confident expression of self. I am clear on my direction, my boundaries, and my purpose; compassionate, mindful, and intentional with my actions and words.

I now have the honour to serve by providing support and guidance to men (and women, and however one identifies) to help reconcile and reclaim their Divine Masculine essence. We *all* can have it ALL. Scarcity and lack are faulty projections of an outdated and misaligned reality. These limiting societal structures have kept us from the realization of who we truly are, and it is time to rise up and take back our sovereignty. I am here to help usher in a new way of being, where the Divine Masculine steps forward and lifts up the Divine Feminine in order to govern this *New Earth*—together.

I am.
I am.
I am anything I choose.
I am anything I focus on.

Because
I am infinite.
I am the universe.
I am everything.
I am you and you are me.
I see myself in the reflection of your eye.
We are one.
We are everything.
We are.

Plant medicine has played a role in my awakening process, but it is not the sole cause. I have had just as profound revelations through breathwork and other meditative activities. When I say that *you are the answer*, I know this to be true because I have experienced the infinite within myself without any additional substance. Conversely, fasting is another powerful practice in which I believe that *when we go without, we can go within*. Ultimately, all of these wonderful modalities are simply tools to assist us in tapping into our truest nature. All of this is within YOU.

There is something to be said for being in alignment as well. We live in a world where there are so many contributing factors that take us away from our highest selves—a way of being where we are able to access these elevated states of consciousness with more ease. In my process of connecting with my higher self (it's been a gradual one), I have become very mindful of what I put in my body—from the food and drink that I ingest (I've been vegan for over a year and a half, and rarely drink anymore), to the products I use on my body (your skin is the largest organ and absorbs whatever you put on it). Additionally, what I say and think (our words are spells, and we become our thoughts), what I watch, read and listen to (there's more out there than the mainstream would like you to believe), as well as the company I keep (they say you are the sum of the five people that you spend the most time with). Those around you should be adding to your growth, cheering you on, and giving you love—I am so fortunate to be amongst big dreamers and doers who constantly inspire, encourage, and motivate me. The one, who I have, by far, spent the most time with over this incredible and expansive period is my amazing partner, Audra. Her nature, presence, and support have enabled me to step into the man that I am. With her, I have been able to transform the way I show up—with stronger integrity, steadfast consistency, empowered self-confidence, unwavering trust, in addition to emotional intelligence and healthy communication. Our evolution as a couple has actually resulted in others seeking us out for support. It has been such a testament for us to be of service in this way, even when in some cases it has been to simply *be* "us." In a world that often perpetuates unhealthy relationship dynamics, we, Audra and myself, feel blessed to share the ways that our partnership is built on a foundation of love, trust, respect, and honour.

I am eternally grateful for our paths to have crossed and intertwined the way in which they have.

On that note of the inspirational Feminine, I have been cultivating, literally and figuratively, my relationship with Mother Earth by ways of gardening over the past several years. This process has taught me so much—how to plan; how to develop the land; how to enrich soil; how to plant seeds; how to be patient; how to nourish growth; how to operate with love and care; how to listen and observe; how to make sacrifices in order to facilitate growth; how to appreciate and enjoy the fruits of my labour; how to deal with loss and disappointment; to know where my food comes from; to harvest diligently; to work hard when it is needed and when to sit back and relax; to make the most of the time that I am given in the short growing season; to prepare for the winter and for the less than ideal times; to let it all go and start all over again.

Working with the earth has taught me about so much more than just gardening. This has been a metaphor and lesson for life. I have grown to embrace my natural essence, as we are all just that—Nature. After all of these years, now with a bigger plot and a deeper relationship, I am being called into further connection with Her, and I am excited to see where this journey leads. If we can impart the mantra "as above, so below" to the popular saying "the sky's the limit", maybe we can begin to understand the incredible gift that our precious Mother Earth truly is.

LOVE HER. HONOUR HER.

In bringing this to a close, my work is not complete, nor will it ever end. I am the work of a lifetime. We all are, each and every one of us, our own life's work. I continue to learn, expand, and practice. That's what life is—practice. Practice for what? The next lifetime? I don't know. But what I do know is that every day that I wake up with breath in my lungs, I get to do it all over again. At times this can sound daunting; another perspective is one of opportunity—*wow, what do I GET to do today?* What a privilege! Maybe I do the same thing as yesterday, or maybe I decide to completely reinvent myself—the beauty is that it is my choice to make. As it is yours, and it's never too late, or *too* anything—it just ... is. And it *is* what YOU make of it.

For the longest time, I had felt that there was something more.

Now I know that there is, and it has been inside of me all along.

If you are hearing this call...

... it is time to answer it.

I am sending you so much love in the pursuit of your truth, your story, and your answers.

They all lie within.

Matty.

ABOUT THE AUTHOR
MATTY RYCE

Matty Ryce is a conscious coach who advocates and teaches self-awareness and integrated living. He embodies the weaving of the archetypal spectrum of sacred feminine and divine masculine while encouraging deep enquiry of the self. Alongside tending to his garden and cultivating experiences through music, Matty believes and supports the transformational capacity we *all* have to heal the mind, body, and spirit.

You can connect with him on:
Instagram: MattyRyce
Facebook: Modern Masculine

MICHAEL DOYLE

THE JOURNEY INWARD: THE NOT SO OBVIOUS PATH TO SELF-MASTERY

INTRODUCTION

So many pieces of my nights were missing. I'd wake feeling tired, hungover, and depressed. What happened last night? Did I play my third set? How did I get home? On the outside, I was the life of the party. They loved how I rocked the stage with my high energy and ability to consume ridiculous amounts of alcohol during my shows. However, on the inside, I was lost, sad, and lacking clarity or direction. I was overweight, living an unhealthy lifestyle, and felt deeply stuck.

We are never really stuck. Everything is energy and energy is always moving. The reason we feel stuck is because we are stuck in our thoughts, beliefs, emotions, and actions. The second we change even one of our daily habits we start to create a new outcome. Yes, life is never a straight line and as they say, calm seas don't make great sailors, but life is somehow... always happening for us. I can say with 100% certainty that whatever your soul is seeking, is seeking you.

You see, I have been feeling called for a while now to start sharing my personal story to guide and empower others to take their lives to the next level. I realize, no two journeys are the same but there are many parallels to igniting your soul's calling. I know you can overcome all of life's adversities and start living the life you know deep down you were meant to live. This chapter is your invitation to trek the most important path we can ever take in life... The Journey Inward.

THE STRUGGLE

In life, all of us have times of joy, sorrow, tears, laughter, struggle, fun, and every other possible emotion and experience in between. My earliest memory of deep pain and struggle was when my sister Darlene and her friend Karen were hit and killed by a drunk driver. I was only 10 years old and although it was 37 years ago now, I can still vividly remember that day unfolding. I remember literally feeling the pain my mom and dad were experiencing and trying to be the "strong one" and hold a space that would support them. Looking back, I rarely allowed myself to cry and unconsciously developed a habit of not processing negative emotions and became a giver while being blocked to receive.

This pattern continued into my relationships as I grew older, and I would always try to be the helper or fixer. I would give, give and then give some more until I lost myself in the process. Eventually, the pain of that dynamic would become too much, and the relationship would end. Guess what I did next... I'd re-create the same dynamic in a new relationship. You see nothing was changing on the inside so I would simply repeat the pattern. I feel relationships are our greatest teachers and can serve us for accelerated growth if we are open to being the observer of our experience while honoring the lessons within the dynamic.

The timing of me writing this is another aligned synchronicity. I recently completed an old pattern and cycle in my romantic relationships. I had a very profound karmic soul-mate connection with an amazing woman. During our relationship, I experienced love at a cosmic level, challenges, growth, and most importantly healing.

This relationship guided me back to me, as I learned to set new boundaries and start loving myself at a deeper level. Love is not something we must seek, for love is what we are.

As I think about some of my obstacles and aha moments, I feel my battle with alcohol is a very important one as it sparked much of my growth, healing, and expansion. I struggled with drinking for almost two decades. I loved to go on long binges and at times drink around the clock. Even after letting myself go to where I weighed over 200 pounds and woke up one morning in a drunk tank, I continued to drink. Thankfully on April 24th, 2010, I had that moment of clarity.

I was sitting on the floor playing with my son Timothy. He was only 14 months old at the time and I felt I didn't have the energy or attention span to give him that he deserved. I felt guilty and thought, "What kind of a role model am I going to be for my son if I keep living my life like this?" Looking back this was the day that I surrendered the struggle on a deeper level. I asked for help from a higher power, and I got that help... Everything in life comes down to a moment of clarity where we get to make a choice. My decision to no longer drink would prove to be a quantum moment in my soul's ascension.

THE PILOT LIGHT

We rarely connect the dots while we are in it but rather can always connect them when we get to look back at our journey. I never consciously tried to do this but I slowly replaced my drinking with fitness and nutrition. Getting my health in check would prove to be one of the catalysts on my road to self-mastery.

Having said this, I do feel the actual pilot light to my expansion was lit during a weekend retreat I attended in Bellingham Washington. The event was called The Holy Relationship and was facilitated by

Sandy Levey-Lunden. I am forever grateful for Sandy and this course she created based on the principles in "A Course In Miracles." During the retreat, we learned a powerful process for clearing ego thoughts called, "The Power of Clearing." There were many healing and uplifting moments, but one experience, stayed very vividly in my mind. I remember the trees, the smells, the sunshine, and where I sat while the facilitator helped guide this amazing three-step process. Once we got to the final stage of the clearing, I was asked to say just three words... "I am innocent." I sat there shaking and crying uncontrollably. I had taped into a deep energetic block or belief, and it was holding on tight. My whole body shook and after what felt like forever, I said "I AM INNOCENT". It is hard to put into words what a powerful release this was. I felt happier, lighter, and now realize an enormous weight was lifted off me in that instant.

I feel it is important to mention that although we will have quantum moments in life and experience great growth it is key, we continue to make time to do the much-needed inner work. I have done countless healing sessions and tried many modalities. We must ensure we are going beneath the surface and getting to the root causes for true healing.

For change to occur in our lives, we must shift to a higher state of consciousness. A shift is at an energetic level internally and hence very powerful. As Albert Einstein said, "we cannot solve our problems with the same level of thinking that created them." It took several awakening moments before I was even aware that what I was experiencing was positive expansion and developing my self-awareness. I am glad that my exposure to a course in miracles lit what was to be the pilot light to my spiritual ascension.

THE AWAKENING

During my awakening, I went through several time periods that you may have heard called, "Dark night of the soul." During these times you will go through the "void," expanding your awareness while elevating your consciousness. I firmly believe life is truly about raising our vibration and expanding our consciousness. Everything we experience is not about economics, borders, religion etc, but simply a reflection of where the frequency of the collective consciousness is currently vibrating.

I believe we are in an exciting time to be a soul on this earth having a human experience. Mother Gaia is healing and fully supporting the ascension from 3-D (separate) to 5-D (unity) consciousness. A New Earth is well into motion, and I believe unity is closer than many people may currently perceive. The love of power is being replaced by the Power of Love. It has been said to know thyself and you shall know the Universe and the Gods. I feel this world pandemic (the real pandemic is fear) has gifted many of us the time to truly journey inward. People are waking up and realizing how much we are on autopilot; on a course, we did not plot for ourselves. Our belief systems and belief in ourselves can completely change the trajectory of our lives. We must first remember we are all Alchemists.

I have experienced so many moments during my awakening, but I feel the most powerful one for me is about love. Love is infinite and in the "Absolute," there is only love. God is love, is in everything, and is omnipresent. My relationship with "God," has been an interesting journey. I am neither for nor against any religions however I feel although they all hold some universal truths, they are all skewed by human beliefs, perceptions, and personal filters. It has been my experience that God and Religion are not the same things. I share my truth and inner "knowings" to empower those who seek to fully know thyself. I am not looking to convince anyone and ask that they all go inward for their answers. Everything you seek is already inside of you, waiting in the ether to be seen, activated, and created. If I was to attempt to define my beliefs and knowing as yours, I am making others wrong and I don't believe in creating more silos but rather help them find the truths that lie deep within themselves. We are all one and not separate from each other, nature, animals, the cosmos but collectively a part of this beautiful dance of unified consciousness.

I have had times of much struggle, of bliss, of love, of fun, of sadness, and every emotion in between. I believe we all experience times of unconsciously going through our routines and habitual habits. The auto-pilot mode often defaults to a setting called a fixed mindset. Fear has at times nearly paralyzed me and stopped me in my tracks. Yet, fear has also fueled me towards my moments of breakthrough and transformation. As I continue to remember and awake to what truly is, I am tapped into the source, God, the quantum field, the ether. This divine matrix is an infinite energy source that fuels all creation. The dream of the planet is created collectively through all spiritual beings that are currently living the human experience. Our souls have chosen this journey. The process of growing, healing, and expanding for me is an amazing experience.

As we journey towards self-mastery, we find it leads us once again to the illusion of self. There is no self as we connect to our true essence. From this beautiful place of awareness, we can serve from a higher place that always is for the greater good. Zen, Taoism, Samadhi are all fundamentally a way of being that can lead you to live your Dharma.

Following a very deep guided group meditation a brief poem channeled through me and although this was over two years ago, every time I read it, I feel it is fitting for my current experience. Our soul will always seek fuller expression and I hope these words become a mantra to guide and support you.

"A new powerful chapter in my spiritual awakening has begun. I fully let go of all limiting and negative beliefs. I fully ignite my light for the higher good of all. True abundance is flowing to me effortlessly. I am joyful, present, and fully alive."

Fully understanding and feeling the power of love during my awakening I once wrote a short prayer to the Universe and feel to share it here as it is about leading with love. Love is infinite positive energy so why not intentionally Lead with Love.

-Prayer to the Universe
"Thank you, Universe, for your greater plan. I fully surrender any need to control and peacefully rest with certainty knowing all is well. I choose to move forward with love, passion, and purpose knowing your guidance is with me. Your plan is better than mine, and I surrender to you fully with joy, love, and much gratitude. I choose to see the world through the eyes of love, I will lead with love, and create from love."

The Change I wish to see in the world can be summarized by a script I wrote a while ago. This was another Divine synchronicity and I realized it would support this chapter.

"The shift and expansion my soul seeks to experience in others is one of deeper connection. The type of connection I speak of involves three layers and eventually aligns you with your natural "Flow State." I believe more and more people are following a call to go inward and explore. It is this journey inward that connects them to their mind, body, and spirit. Mastering your connection with yourself is layer one. When you strengthen this connection, it becomes the doorway to your soul revealing its calling to you. This is layer two and it is a very exciting time because you are becoming fueled by a burning desire to follow and fulfill your passions. In living your soul's calling you discover the illusion of self. You begin to feel and live the oneness of all that is. Now creating from the quantum field, together we will heal the planet."

A FEW OF THE LESSONS I'VE LEARNED

- Acceptance is Peace

We all find ourselves at certain stages in life facing adversity, challenges, or perceived obstacles. We often try to extract a linear progression or reason behind our pain or current situation. We are full of 'should of', 'would of' and 'could of', while replaying all the things we'd do differently; or we blame others, holding on to anger and resentment. In both cases, we are out of alignment. When our happiness is dependent on something or someone outside of ourselves, we are giving away our power.

Where we are currently, is a direct product of every thought we had, every belief we programmed, and every action we took along the way. This may be a hard pill to swallow; the good news is everything happens for a reason.

Time and time again I see so many people turn their pain into their power. To reach a place of acceptance there is a key element of forgiveness required; forgiveness to ourselves and toward others. Many people believe that by forgiving someone, they are saying it's okay. However, what they are really doing is removing the negative energy of anger from their mind, body, and soul. Only then can you place your energy, awareness, and focus on the 'now' while accepting where you are. When we fully accept where we are and take responsibility; it creates a positive shift, and we take back our power, aligning with our true self.

I am grateful to now be at a stage in my life where I feel inflow and in harmony with the Universe. This doesn't mean I never have ups and downs; in actuality, I feel awakened to a level where obstacles rarely take me off course. If something does take me off course, it is never as drastic, or for as long, as it once would have. Why is this? It is because I no longer push against what is; my self-awareness allows me to fully accept. Acceptance is peace.

- Our Thoughts are Powerful

Our thoughts shape our reality period. Yes, there are other factors like our energy, vibration, beliefs, and actions that influence what we create however, everything starts with a thought. Much of what we think about and the associated emotions that follow are largely based on the past.

Starting at birth we use our thoughts to develop many beliefs. As we grow, learn, explore and expand we create self-awareness developing our metacognition. As humans we have been gifted the ability to think about our thoughts. Through this process, we may realize that not all beliefs are supporting our journey. Certain beliefs may have once served us but no longer does, others still serve us while many were never healthy, but we accepted them into our subconscious largely by the age of seven.

Our environment, perceptions, and beliefs about ourselves and the world around us set the stage for our habitual thinking programs. Either consciously or unconsciously we are co-creating with the unified field. The environment we spend time in will influence what we create.

It has been said that Love and Fear are the only two words in the language of the soul. Many people are in a place of fear, and this creates a lower vibration as well as negative thoughts. Creating from this place will always attract people and experiences that are unwanted. While creating from Love will consistently gift you people and experiences that you will enjoy.

We are indeed our biggest obstacle in life, but the good news is we are also our greatest asset. Which one you fuel the most, determines the quality of your life. We intrinsically understand there is power in knowing thyself.

In studies of human behavior and our thoughts, there is scientific proof that all thoughts have corresponding neurological and chemical effects within our body. All our decisions in life come down to making a choice. If most of your thoughts are not helping you create the life you want, then choose to "change your thoughts."

> "When you change the way you look at things, the things you look at change." - Wayne Dyer

- The Power of Shifting Your Focus

When dealing with our energy, thoughts, beliefs, language, and habits it is a game-changer when we learn to shift our focus. This can help us go from a negative pattern to a positive pattern. Intellectually we know being on the positive side of the scale is beneficial for us in life. We are all programmed with habits, beliefs, and paradigms that sometimes can keep us feeling stuck. When we are stuck in negative patterns, we are creating more of what we don't want. As I previously mentioned consciously or unconsciously we are creating our experience.

Our Energy plays a major role in how we show up each day. Are we clear and excited? Are we feeling full of energy? Are we feeling tired and very low energy? We all experience both sides of this spectrum, but we have control over where our energy levels are going to be most days.

Our thoughts are powerful and over time help us create our reality. No one has, nor ever will create something positive using a negative mindset. Successful people learn to spend only 5% of their time on the problem and 95% on creating solutions. Where are your thoughts most of the time?

Never underestimate the power of our belief in ourselves. Developing our ability to visualize our goals is key. We must create it in the mindscape first. Neville in The Power of Awareness wrote, "you must assume the feeling of the wish fulfilled." We can be wired for an amazing life but many of us will have to re-pattern the neuro-pathways to create that life. Bob Proctor says, "you will never exceed your self-image." Do you believe in your ability to do the things you want to do?

The language we use on a regular basis is so important. It took me a while to fully grasp this concept. If you say I want to get out of debt, you may think this is a positive statement. However, your focus is still on debt therefore you attract more of it. Instead, say I will continue to increase my income. The focus is now on creating more income which will of course remove the debt over time.

Nate Green said, "Habits make us, and habits break us." A constructive habit will support us while a de-constructive habit does the opposite. It took me a while, but I replaced my drinking habit with better fitness and nutrition habits. We all have the power to replace our negative habits with positive ones. I believe success is achieved by completing simple effective daily habits consistently over time.

- Our Health is Our Wealth

We either make time for our wellness or eventually, we will be forced to make time for our sickness and disease. Dis-Ease is always created at an energetic level before it is realized in our physical reality. When we are out of alignment for too long it will over time translate into our day-to-day experiences as physical manifestations.

It has been my experience working with countless clients that we all hit a point in our lives where we must put ourselves first. I don't mean in a selfish or egotistical way but in an empowering way where we are being fueled daily. Learning to fuel our mind, body, and spirit daily is key but it takes awareness, intention, focused action, and practice. I love the analogy that we can't pour from an empty cup. I feel this is accurate, but it wasn't until a good friend of mine shared something her mentor had told her. She said we are never pouring from our cup. It's about self-care and filling our cup first. Basically, we learn to fill our cup so consistently that we are always giving still, but from the overflow.

Self-investment is not only the best thing we can do for ourselves but also the people around us. The more we grow, the greater capacity we have to serve others. We can only help people to the level we have learned to help ourselves.

There are things I do daily, weekly and monthly that help me show up the way I do for both myself and others. I spoke during a World Fitness Expo at a Leadership conference and every leader over the three-day event basically said leading themselves first was their secret to being an effective leader.

Most of us know the things we can do to stay healthier. Eat less, stay away from processed foods, stay active and exercise a few days a week, get enough rest...you get the picture. What works for me may not work for you so try different modalities, fitness routines, and foods and learn what works for you. Some of my core habits are Running, working out, daily green shake, breath work, mobility and core work, and time in nature just to name a few. A good habit to develop that can increase your chances of having a solid foundation is establishing a good morning routine. We all get the same number of hours a day to get things done and a routine will help you stay more consistent.

- The Power of Forgiveness & Gratitude

There are going to be times in life where learning to forgive ourselves and others will be necessary. Well, it is a choice, but forgiveness is required if we want to grow and move beyond our current reality and experience new levels of flow and fulfillment. I mentioned earlier in this chapter that my sister Darlene was hit and killed by a drunk driver. I was so mad at the driver and for years I held onto this anger and wanted to hurt him. It wasn't until much healing, growth and several layers of awakening I was able to fully see things differently. I met the driver of the car in a vivid dream one night. I saw the sadness in his eyes and felt the pain in his heart. Instead of being mad or finally getting even I just looked deeply into his eyes and allowed myself to feel what he was feeling. I finally spoke and said, "it's okay, I forgive you." He looked at me and started to cry, then I started to cry, and I gave him a hug. Then all I could see was beautiful white light and the moment was gone. It wasn't until years later that I realized I had experienced a profound quantum healing during my dream that night.

I have faced other fears and challenges but can fully say I am grateful for all of my experiences. No matter where you are in your journey or what you are experiencing right now, I know there is someone somewhere who would love to have what you do right now. Being grateful for what we have while we work towards the things, we want is so important. Forgive, give thanks, learn the lessons and move on with excitement for what the future holds. When we are able to focus on the good and fully feel gratitude in our hearts, we will create more experiences to be grateful for.

- Harnessing Flow while balancing Our Growth

I briefly talked about Inner Synergy in my book At The Helm. I later realized that what I was experiencing and describing in my book was something called "Flow-State." Musicians, athletes, writers, authors, and many others relate to this state. It's when you are super focused on whatever it is you are doing or creating and fully in the moment. Time disappears while every cell in your body along with your thoughts, emotions, and actions are energetically aligned. You see, our minds can serve us or control us, but it is a choice. Either consciously or unconsciously we are co-creating with the Quantum Field and the people we engage with along the way. When we lead with our hearts and use our minds to create there is beautiful magic that happens. Our thoughts, emotions, words, and actions become vibrationally in sync and are in perfect resonance. This creates flow. Flow state is at the foundation of all alchemy and creating from this place will always serve the greater good. Water is our life source and is at its highest vibration when it is flowing. Our physical body as humans is largely made up of water therefore when we are experiencing a flow state we too are at our highest vibration. We are literally tapping into the universal life source that flows through all creation.

However, as an expert in human potential and peak performance, I do want to mention that we must balance our time and ensure we are moving beyond our comfort zone as well. I love flow state big time, but I know we are comfortable in the flow state and therefore not growing.

- Letting The Fear Fuel You

I am fascinated with fear and learned that fear serves a great purpose in our lives. Successful people don't remove fear rather they learn to manage it. In fact, with enough practice, you can let the fear now fuel you instead of stopping you.

I faced my fear of deep water by deciding to complete a sprint triathlon. I trained in the Arctic for nine months and in 2011 I completed two events that summer. It took commitment, support, and consistent training but our obstacles are always opportunities to grow. The real challenge even on the day of the events was in my head while in the water. I chose to move past my fears.

I also had a huge fear of public speaking. Although as a professional musician I was very comfortable on stage if you took away my guitar, I was a nervous wreck. I decided to face this fear and joined toastmasters for a few months. I then spoke at a momondays London event and within six months I was the new co-host. I am now often inflow while giving a keynote or motivational talk.

I have overcome other fears and obstacles but it all initially began with a choice followed by a commitment. I basically asked myself the following question. Who do I have to become, to do the things I want to do? Once this is clear, simply set goals and start taking action. Everything we seek is always on the other side of our fears.

"Let fear become the motivational jet fuel that propels you at lightning speed towards your goals."

CONCLUSION

I am fascinated with human potential, peak performance, and what really drives us in life. I have a healthy obsession with flow-state and consciousness itself. My Dharma is to collectively raise the greater consciousness of the world through connection and collaboration. At a micro-level, it is about empowering others. I exist to unlock the potential in people, organizations, and specifically their leadership teams. I am an expert in getting everyone in the same boat, rowing in the same direction, excited to be there, know where they are going, and clear on how they individually contribute to the team and vision. As a speaker, author, and coach my books, workshops, courses, free webinars, etc... are all designed to unlock the infinite potential that is waiting to be fully activated inside of you.

In closing out this chapter I will share with you a poem I recently wrote. I feel it aligns with my overall message that we all must trek the journey inward to fully thrive in life. Your time is now...

The Journey Inward
The Journey Inward brings awakening near
Connecting with God, releasing all fear
The power of NOW brings alignment and peace

I lead with love, with all those I meet
I surrender today, in every way
I trust in knowing, my soul knows the way
I am Clarity, Flow, Joy, Love, and Light
Always fueling, my soul into flight
I am that I am, and "all" that has been
For we are all one, in all the unseen
Love is the answer, this Truth will stay
For its Divine light, that's lighting the way

ABOUT THE AUTHOR
MICHAEL DOYLE

Imagine a world where everyone supports their own personal growth and the expansion of others. My Dharma is to collectively raise the greater consciousness of the world through connection and collaboration. I exist to unleash the potential in others.

I fully believe everyone has the power to follow their dreams and discover the deeper purpose of their life. I went from being exhausted, overweight, drinking in excess and feeling stuck to thriving. A decade later after much personal and professional growth, I dedicate my life to serving others.

I help my clients by leading them to new levels of Clarity and Flow in their life, business, and careers. I do this by always developing and using my gifts as a speaker, author and coach. I'm an expert in human potential, peak performance and what really drives us in life! My healthy obsession with flow-state and consciousness itself continues to drive me forward as I further develop my innate ability to unlock human potential.

If you are feeling stuck or are simply ready for the next level your soul is seeking, I am your personal GPS that will support your unique journey from where you are to where you truly want to go.

More importantly, I ensure the journey is more fulfilling while you work towards achieving your deeper "soul's calling."

Social Media Links –
Website: https://doyleitin.com/
Facebook : https://www.facebook.com/doyleitin/
Instagram: https://www.instagram.com/doyleitin/
LinkedIn: https://www.linkedin.com/in/michael-doyle-43025a103/

6

SPIRITUAL NAME: RANIN-RAWA
GOVERNMENT NAME: GEOFF LARDEN

Warriors journey back to the heart centre

I knew in my heart there must be more to this life. The false sense of well-being drinking profusely and taking home random women to sleep with every weekend no longer does the trick. I've reached the pinnacle of the narcotics business and have all the money in the world to nurture my vices. I live by my own rules. I don't need to punch a clock and live some mundane life. The despair of emptiness is killing me inside. I'm a f*cking man. I should be able to buck up and deal with my emotions. If I could just let people in, all my problems would be solved. Where do I begin? I can't ask for help, can I?

Two decades of being deeply entrenched in the narcotics business had taken its toll on me. The mask I wore to hide my emotions had grown so thick that I didn't recognize the man in the mirror anymore. I kept all my loved ones at an arm's length to protect them from knowing the depth of the line of work I was in. Well, if I'm being honest, it was more out of fear of them knowing the pain I was coping with inside. My nervous system was a wreck from the decade-long battle with suppressing all my emotions. I thought I could do it all on my own. I had no idea how to ask for help. I was the leader of my crew, tough as nails and mired in a knee-deep depression that my ego prevented me from admitting. Rock bottom had left me draining the last drop of alcohol in a dungy after hours, sniffing cocaine and blowing money on the poker table every weekend of my life. My dick stopped working for the sexual partners I had. It was high time I broke the cycle of insanity and admitted I needed help.

I woke up one morning after a long night of boozing, desperate for help. My mouth tasted like an ashtray, clouds blurred my thoughts and my head felt like a sledge hammer had been taken to it. The insane amounts of booze I consumed to help cope with my thoughts and the anvil of guilt I carried no longer did the trick. I googled "shrink near me"—the first of many decisions I reflect on that saved my life. I was playing Russian roulette daily by being involved in the narcotics industry. In this line of work, you run the risk daily of getting robbed by low lives trying to take what they can't have, someone snitching on you and getting yourself landed in jail, or even worse being killed over a deal gone wrong. I yearned to leave "the game" behind me.

I walked into the psychiatrist's office feeling like Tony Soprano. All the voices in my head were firing on all cylinders. "You lil b***h!"—"man the F up and deal with your shit!"—"How the f*uck is this university graduate gonna help you?" The ego desperately was hanging onto power. I overrode these voices and began a journey of deep self-exploration. For the first time in my life, I opened up, and boy did I release a ton of emotions from the years of emotional constipation. I began to take accountability for the life that was no longer working for me, and boy, was it ever a messy process. This marked a stretch of my life I know as "the great turning", getting dealt death blow after death blow to an ego that had been having its way for some time. I had repressed depression for so long that I had no choice but to let it run all over me. I opened up to my friends and family about my struggles with depression and alcoholism and sugar-coated the depth of the line of work I was in with my family. All in all, tremendous progress was being made.

One particular session with my psychiatrist made me aware of how many daddy issues I had been carrying with me—blaming my father for all the emotional constipation—blaming him for why I left home at a young age and got into narcotics. My childhood memories consisted of being paralyzed by fear over upsetting him and the reason I couldn't articulate my emotions. I had created this narrative that if I could just feel free to express myself to him, it would have some domino effect, and I would be liberated! Well, not quite.

Walking back from my shrink's office, which happened to be blocks from my parents' house, I made a choice. I grew the courage to face my father. A deep wave of anxiety came over me. My entire life I feared my fathers demeanor. Standing on the front steps of my parents' home, I stood breathing heavily in an attempt to compose myself. My sister, hearing me all the way from the backyard, came to check on me. "Are you Ok?" She asks. I composed myself and held back the tears, "yes, I gotta go talk to dad." Walking up the stairs to his office, the emotions become overwhelming, and I burst out in tears. So much fear around opening up to him. "Am I going through with this?" I thought to myself. "F@ck it, what do you have to lose?" was the response. I stepped into his office, distraught, lost and needed his help. "Dad, I gotta talk to you." Seeing me in tears, he looks up, seemingly annoyed at me, and asks, "Geoffrey, are you going to jail again?" I laughed out loud, "no, dad, I'm depressed, and I need your help. I need you to be my father." The craziest, perhaps most transformative event unfolded as my father, this incredibly stoic man whom I had only witnessed shed a tear at his mother's funeral, joined me in my release of pent-up energies and cried. He shared with me he had struggled with depression his entire adult life, and only in recent years, at the ripe age of 70, had he been able to cope with his thoughts, and if it wasn't for my mother, he didn't know if he would have made it. Wow! I would never have known had I not had the courage to come clean with my challenges. I realized on a deeper level the profound strength in vulnerability. My opening up gave him permission to do the same. All my resentment alchemized into compassion. I understood why he was so on edge growing up. I wasn't the only one suffering in silence. He went from being the villain to being my hero as this man worked upwards of 60 hrs/week, raising four children, all the while coping with depression during an era where men didn't have the options to open up about these challenges. I made a choice that day that I wasn't going to go on suffering in silence until my later years, and it became my life's mission to do some heavy lifting for myself and my forefathers.

Alcohol had me by the balls, and it took a brother/business associate to test my willpower one night at a dinner gathering for me to get off the booze. "Two shots and a beer!" I ordered after crushing a massive steak dinner and six beers. My brother, having little faith in my ability to stop drinking, says in front of my other brothers, "I'll give you $50,000 if you can quit drinking for six months, starting tomorrow." This was the test my ego needed. So I did it. I quit drinking for six months, and it was torture. My whole identity was connected to drinking and being the life of the party and I couldn't wait for the bet to end. I held a welcome back party to drinking with all my friends there and gave a stirring speech declaring my love for the bottle. I came back with a vengeance. My body and spirit had other plans for me. Anxiety kicked up in a major way, and I enrolled in a transcendental meditation course to help combat it. I choose to think the meditation was helping to alleviate stressors put onto my nervous system, which was tremendously challenging.

At this point, a spiritual advisor I began working with offered that I consider taking part in a ten-day silent retreat called vipassana, upon reflection proved to be another choice that may have saved my life. The program showed me just how much resentment and blame I had been carrying for all the perceived wrongdoings towards me in my life. The ego wants to deflect blame and never take accountability. For seven days, I listened to this deep victim voice, blaming the world for my issues. "This person fuc*ed you over in this deal", "damn father never listened to me". The voice was so powerful I couldn't detach from it and felt I was it. This ever incessant chattering victimizing voice was having a field day. Finally on the seventh day I had a breakthrough and found myself being able to separate from the voice and not be it. I walked out of the meditation hall and it was as if a veil had been lifted from my field. My senses were tremendously heightened, I observed a butterfly fluttering overhead, the sun peeking through the trees and glistening off of a rock and small pieces of plastic tied to trees that felt out of place all at the same time. The voice was gone…temporarily. I learnt the voice is not me, and I could sit with my thoughts and not be them. I had been so consumed by my four cell phones and a lifestyle that I could never sit still. For the first time in my life, I felt content sitting in silence.

The vortex, however, was layers deep, and I was far from out of the woodworks. I lost a lover way too young to a slow self-induced drug overdose. I had no idea how much I loved her until she passed. I went on the largest drinking bender of my life, feeling so much guilt for her death. Tears flowed out of me like a waterfall. I know longer gave a shit about the mundane stuff in life and spent the next two months drinking every night, up till 7-8 am half the week at a friend's after-hours with the veil between life and death appearing so thin that I couldn't decipher which dimension I was in. I was losing money by the boatloads from deals gone wrong, and I didn't give a shit. When this bender ended, I was gutted and felt I had hit an entirely new level of rock bottom. Too meek to speak my truths, too hurting to take care of the day-day tasks of life and so emotionally fragile that I holed myself up to avert human connection.

The divine, however, threw me a lifeline. During the two-month debacle, I met a beautiful woman who threw her persistent way and enrolled me in a vision for a movement and a record label called Bold x Centred(BxC)—a social justice movement encouraging humanity to stand bold in their beliefs and stay centred in your hearts, combined with a record label supporting artists whose music inspired humanity. The label would highlight the movement, and the movement would highlight the label. I loved it and decided to invest in it the day after the funeral of the woman I lost.

Pretty symbolic.

This movement gave me a newfound meaning in life, and I began to clean up my act. I mixed business with pleasure and fell in love. We got into action and hosted some events mainly focused on her as an artist. I sunk loads of money into it to try and make it work, neglecting the fact I had no background in running a record label or leading a social justice movement. I played out this huge hero role with her to avert saving myself. What a gift she was, a woman I thought I would spend the rest of my life with. I financed the business, her music career and gave her an apartment in my house to live in.

Then I received another death blow to the ego.

One winter afternoon, I waited in my driveway for my girlfriend as she went back inside to get her coat to walk the dog. "Get on the ground!" I looked over and saw a handful of undercover officers rush my driveway and take a battering ram to the front door. I was caught red-handed. My nonchalant depressive mental state had me breaking the number one rule of "the game". Never keep products in your own house. They found 5000 percocets, an ounce of cocaine, and a few thousand dollars. Enough to land me behind bars for some time. I was already in debt and just lost another $50,000 in product. Within one week, my life and business partner left me and the Bold X Centred movement behind. I was broke, alone, and facing serious time. She was the face and visionary of the movement. All the members of BxC left with her. I was left with a decision. Fold up shop, face the realistic possibility of an extended period behind bars, or buck up, start from scratch and pursue this dream that had become my purpose for living. This movement was all I had. "Fk it, let's do this."

I quickly re-assembled a team and started making a major impact. A BBQ event we hosted in a housing project snowballed into partnering with pro-action police for a weekly drop-in basketball program. Doors started to open. We ran an after-school club, a summer activities camp and began to make a major impact in this underserved community. I turned a bedroom in my home into a music studio to support the label. Progress was being made quickly. I learnt the concept of "surrender" as I daily lived with the awareness I could be doing up to 4 years in jail. I choose to live and not be behind bars already—what a time. I had one foot in this philanthropic life, working with pro-action police, shaking hands with local MPs and community leaders who desired to work with me, all the while having one foot in the underworld funding these projects and paying my lawyer bill. I had wanted out of "the game" for a long time. As my confidence grew and my faith in a higher force strengthened, I made a choice that I look back on as my greatest achievement in life, one month prior to trial.

"Dear God, source, whoever is out there, I'm done. My heart can't do this anymore. I don't know how I'll survive, but I trust. If my life is better spent behind bars for humanity's sake, then I accept that. If it's not, then hook a brother up. Amen." I completely surrendered to the outcome and the potential of doing four years in jail.

Prior to trial, the prosecution threw in the towel as they botched how they obtained the search warrant. I got off on a technicality. I choose to think that there was a trial up there in the heavens, and my genuine shift in direction was the real reason I got off. BxC hosted one last major event, which made a huge impact on the community, not realizing this was the closing curtain for the organization. I had to do me. I took my gift from the universe and never looked back. I folded up shop, put my house up for sale, and said goodbye to the narcotics business for good.

Truth be told, I was tired. I was tired of keeping it together. I was tired of the mental anguish from two decades of being in "the game". I needed a reboot.

So I decided to go on a 3 year journey connecting with some of the oldest tribes in the world, in search of a deeper meaning to this existence. The jungle had been calling me for some time, and the first pit stop led me to the lungs of pachamama, the Amazon rainforest.

I came with two clear intentions. A complete disconnect to reconnect and to re-establish my relationship with Christ. I had pushed out institutional religion and Christ a long time ago due to the perceived injustices done to our first nations brothers and sisters at residential schools under the guise of Christ. I realized Christ had nothing to do with these injustices, and I had no clue how to set out to reconnect with Christ.

I weaved my way through the Amazon, living amongst and being received like family from the Shipibo people. I was given the name Ranin-Rawa, meaning beautiful skin of the earth, rolling thunder, and lightning. A leader of his tribe who takes care of his people. Through sheer divine guidance, I landed in a small Shipibo community living at the governor's home in a town called Paohyun.

"Es mi amigo Ranin-Rawa" the governor says as he introduces me to an audience of over 400 indigenous tribesmen. I waved like the Queen of England. He just completed a speech as he was campaigning to be governor of the entire Ucayali River, which consisted of six small communities. "Bilar!, he says to me and a woman who became a soul sister to me, which means dance in Spanish. I was strong-armed into opening the dance floor with my sister, and we began picking elders out of the crowd to dance with us. I revelled in the moment in sheer awe of how I was guided here. These people, I only saw on the cover of Time Magazine, and now I was going across the Amazon in hollowed-out canoes on a campaign party with the governor. Wild stuff.

Ayusaksa is a plant found in the Amazon that is used in sacred ceremonies facilitated by a shaman to bring healing to deeply buried traumas and pain. I had no intentions of working with this plant medicine, but it found me. And boy, did it push me to the brink of insanity. This medicine is not for the faint of heart.

I lay back in a long boat made from a tree of the amazon in a state of gratitude and exuberance as I listened to the symphony birds, the insects buzzing while taking in the incredible lively colours of orange, pink and neon green from the plants and trees which loomed overhead. Such a lush, rich environment. My shaman had identified an animal spirit living in my throat, and we set out that day to gather barks, roots and leaves for a vapour he said would help clear my throat of this animal spirit. "Rawa, look!" my shaman says in Spanish. He was sifting through a banana leaf with remnants from the concoction the morning after a tremendously maddening ayahuasca journey. Pointing with a stick, he shows me four pure white worms that had come out of my throat. I was beyond myself with disbelief. Every medium or energy worker I saw pointed out trauma around my throat. Self-expression had been a targeted area of development for some time. Now I'm seeing pure white worms come out of my throat. How on earth was the medicine man so intune with the elements of the jungle to produce a vapour specifically to help clear my throat blockages. The incredible wisdom and knowledge of the plant world is completely beyond my comprehension.

My last pit stop had me sitting with a 92 year old shaman from a very powerful lineage of ayahuasqueros I called big poppa Pasquel. His apprentice, a brother from Switzerland, explained that Pasquel works with the energies of the tree of life. Shamans are typically called by a specific plant to work with for healing properties. He explains that the tree of life is a direct connection to Christ's consciousness. I found what my spirit was looking for.

"Marijuana, cocaine?" he said during my first ceremony, as he was able to see the spirit of these plants in my field. I sat doing three ceremonies of a "limpiado", a cleansing of my energetic field prior to him infusing the spirit of the tree of life into my being. The medicine kicked my ass. The entire 22 ceremonies were all about getting me out of my head and into my heart. The ego held on for dear life and had me on the brink of insanity. Every ceremony, I would strip down naked, ripping off energies and entities I was convinced entered my field from the decade of spending every weekend at after hours, sex with multiple women under the influence, my life in narcotics, and consuming copious amounts of "spirits" to numb myself. After about the 16th ceremony, I finally had a pants-on party and began to sit with the uncomfortable thought forms and apparent entities. I realized all this madness was a magnification of my own thoughts. I learned to give love and compassion to the most uncomfortable thoughts and learnt in life. You don't just get to purge out things you don't like. In order to alchemize them, you must shed light on them, work with them and give love and compassion to them. During my last ceremony the shaman called me up to seal off the energetics infused into my being by singing his icaros, medicine songs which carry a frequency for energetic alignment. I felt this gentle wave of energy cascade down my body like a deep cleansing for my soul.

By the end of the journey, I finally felt I could be present in life again. I didn't have to entertain every thought. The greatest advice I received was from the apprentice. "Rawa, never mind the mind, eh! It's not always your friend," he says after I spend so much time mentally dissecting every ceremony. I was a prisoner of the mind no more. By the time I left, I had sat on the bank of the Amazon River, hands glued in prayer, feeling the connection to all of life in sheer awe at the incredible guiding force that landed me here and present to just how powerful manifestors we humans are when intentions are made with purity of heart.

The following winter spirit guided me to connect with an indigenous tribe in the Andes known as the Qeros people. The Qeros are highly regarded as the high priests of the Incan Empire and live17000 feet above sea level and are known to be masters of working with the energies of the spirit world.

I signed up for an extended work exchange program where I learnt a technique of farming called grow bio-intensive farming, which aims at maximizing yield per square foot of land utilizing soil regenerative practices. I took on the role of land manager and led a small team in revitalizing lands that hadn't been arable in some time. The woman who ran the organization married a qeros man whose father facilitated many ceremonies on the lands, asking for support from the heavens in the form of a despacho. An offering to the gods made in a bundle consisting of seeds, grains, coca leaves and sweets.

As fate would have it, another indigenous group of elders happened to be coming thru the sacred valley of Peru. A group known as the Kogi Mammos.

They spend their first 18 years of their lives living in caves, in relative darkness, to learn to commune with the forces of this world. They then become Mamos(enlightened ones). Our small team had the honour of hosting them on the lands.

I witnessed in awe as two groups of wisdom keepers came together to partake in a despacho on the lands. "Send all your prayers into the bundle," our Qeros Paco Juan Gabriel says. We sat in a small group under a makeshift shelter on farm land we were developing surrounded by breathtaking mountains. Vibrant blue waters poured down a waterfall in the near distance. I breathed deeply as the oxygen in the air cleansed my energy field.. What an honour it was to witness and partake in the merging of these two highly regarded spiritual leaders. I found myself visiting sacred sites and making offerings to the waters with the Mamos, and to cap off the journey, I made my way out to the Qeros community with my brother Julian.

As fate would have it, their annual ceremony to honour the gods took place upon my arrival. They wore beautifully designed outfits with vibrant colours and sang and danced all day. Their community reminded me of a scene out of Star Wars Jedi training camp. I walked the lands so high in altitude I stood at the base of a rainbow. They lived with minimal needs, in stone homes with no electricity, and lived primarily on potatoes and emitted the most remarkable radiant light from their faces. To cap off the journey, Juan Gabriel facilitated a Karpi—an energetic initiation that opens up pathways to connect to internal processes, external relationships, and cosmic inspiration.

The day of the Karpi had arrived. I got sick as a dog. Juan Gabriel and his two sons took me up the mountainside of Apu Veronica. These Qeros were strong and like mountain goats. They carried sacks of wood for which to be used in the ceremony. I staggered across the terrain and could barely hold a water bottle. Something energetically in me was resistant and doing whatever possible to prevent me from the initiation. I imagine the ego, holding onto power. I stopped often and relieved myself out the backside feeling in and out of consciousness. This group of Qeros Pacos performed a karpi, infusing my field with the energies of the Apu and the cosmos. I could barely make it back down the mountain as I was walloped with flu-like symptoms. I persevered and completed my right of passage. I felt a deep reminder of who my greatest teachers are, mother earth, father sky and the elementals.

The last pit stop on my journey of reconnecting with the origins of mankind led me to the heart of Africa, Kenya. I had made a promise to a young woman I had been sponsoring for the previous decade to visit her, and I volunteered with the organization I sponsored her through called Living Positive Kenya (LPK). I spent the first three months implementing the bio-intensive farming technique on lands the organization stewarded and connecting to the organization. LPK empowers women who are HIV positive and puts them into a three-phase program that gives them the emotional support to see value in their lives again, followed by practical life skills which they parlay into an entrepreneurial business. This organization makes an absolutely remarkable impact. I heard the most remarkable stories of heartbreak and resilience from these sisters who were often left by their partners, blamed for carrying the virus, and shamed from their communities. So many women as young as 16 resigned to the fact they would never find a decent partner and would rather be alone. So much disdain towards men. They're abusive, cheaters, emotionally unavailable, and all they do is drink. I understood all too well the suffering inside that leads a man to these behaviours, and upon seeing the tremendous divide of understanding amongst men and women, I set out to shoot a documentary on uncovering the conditioning of the sexes amongst our oldest tribes. I barely knew how to work my camera, but the intention was set, and I again watched the universe provided the rest.

I enrolled a sister, Faith, a young Kenyan woman, to travel with me by bus across the country, connecting with indigenous tribes and capturing footage on route to a place called Lake Turkana. The only guiding force being a tattoo on my upper right arm of a young warrior girl whom I was told upon arrival was from the Turkana tribe. Clearly, that was where I was meant to go. With absolutely zero plans, we set out on a remarkable journey connecting with some of the world's oldest tribes. We were welcomed into the Massai and Samburu tribes with open arms and experienced firsthand the huge gap of understanding between men and women.

The distorted masculine, not men, had been idolized for centuries and had been drowning out the feminine energies of compassion, love and unity. I felt deep compassion towards the stoic Kenyan man —boys as young as five were trained to be warriors and weaned off their mother's nurturing. At 15, they go through extreme rites of passage ceremonies to prove their warrior abilities by killing a lion or a crocodile and feats of incredible danger. They are given lessons on how to handle a woman's wavering emotions, taught never to show weakness, and how to be a warrior for the tribe. They are circumcised, and if they flinch, they are banished from the tribe as well as their mother for raising weak children. I found them to be some of the kindest men, and felt the pain they must endure for living through generations of not being conditioned to feel their emotions. To live in deeper states of self love. Women go through their own rite of passage ceremony traditionally involving female genital mutilation, which has been banned but still very much practiced in secrecy. They are groomed to serve a man and are often exchanged in barter by their families to be a wife by a husband who chooses them, having no say in the matter. The incredible resilience, strength of character and the compassion these women displayed inspired me greatly. We captured some incredible footage regarding the huge disparity between men and women.

We weaved our way across Kenya and landed at a town called Loyangalani in Lake Turkana. Upon arrival, an incredibly well-marketed fear pandemic spread across the world called Covid-19. Everyone had been rushing to catch emergency flights home. I made the choice to brave it out and stay. As the world's collapsing as I knew it, I was back to where it all began living in huts made of cow dung with one of the oldest tribes in the world in a region known as the cradle of civilization as the oldest skeletons in the world had been found here. The tribe lived primarily off of meat, blood, and milk. They bartered for staple foods and had little use for money. Their livestock acted as their banking system and had little to no use for material objects. I spent the next three months quarantined in Turkana and welcomed to live with a family free of charge as the world unravelled.

The unbelievable amount of love I was shown at every stop of my journey was remarkable. The Kenyan people being some of the kindest people I've had the honour of connecting with—such deep teaching of unconditional love, compassion, and support from the universe. Every step of my journey was divinely guided. I had zero plans, and every time fear arose, I stepped into it and was rewarded. The people's connection to the earth is so present on their faces—the simplicity of their lifestyles I loved. To me, they were rich. Most people had a plot of land to farm on, access to water, and weren't swimming in debt from taxes. I weighed in on if I wanted to return to Canada, and very well may not have if it wasn't for a dream I had that

I would lose the property I was stewarding over building permit issues I had not yet dealt with.

The teachings and knowledge gained through my journeys living amongst indigenious tribes greatly inspired me to create an intentional, off grid, living community which seeks to develop a symbiotic relationship to pachamama on the lands I have been honoured to steward. My passion now revolves around cultivating more skills towards stewardship of mother earth. Learning the native plants of my land and the healing properties they hold. Educating myself on regenerative farming practices, fostering skills like building solar dehydrators, root cellars and growing mushrooms feeds my desires for stimulation. Daily routines of breathwork, yoga, singing and detoxifying in a sauna cleanse and elevates my spirit. Tribe consciousness is now embedded in my genetic makeup with the recognition of the need to step out of the I and into the we. Breaking down old paradigms of needless competition, hierarchy and greed and embracing a lifestyle that supports cooperative living, working to each other's strength and putting our energies towards a reciprocal lifestyle that honours all living creatures. The lands I nurture, nurtures me back in return.

I'm very grateful for the upbringing I had. Living in Toronto and being exposed to the diversity this magnificent city offers has taught me we truly are all one. I didn't even know what racism was until my teenage years as my parents openly welcomed any friends of differing races I brought home to play with. My childhood was incredible. My parents implemented in me my love of nature at a young age with annual canoe trips, getting involved in beavers, cubs and scouts and spending copious amounts of time outside of the city. After bringing healing to the childhood wounds, which no one is exempt from, I'm filled with memories of the abundance of love I received from my family, my cousins and aunts and uncles. My father taught me Integrity, honesty and hard work and gave his entire life to raising his family. My mother is a complete angel who incessantly takes care of her loved one's, and an incredibly talented woman who gave every ounce of her being into providing us an amazing upbringing. However emotional intelligence was something I have had to learn on my own, humbly admitting is an unfolding journey.

I rebelled against society's norms since youth and pushed back against any institutional ways of thinking. Too much control and manipulation of one's consciousness. Radical, free thinking humans being a threat to institutions founded on control, manipulation and concentrated powers. Self sovereignty is vital for the growth of humanity and my path is to step outside of systems that are showing it's vulnerability.

I understand the distorted masculine. Emotionally unavailable, seeking meaning externally and the coping mechanisms needed to give themselves permission to feel life. I feel like I understand the distorted feminine. Too passive to speak their truths, too emotionally fragile to let people in, and too disempowered to realize their full potential.

The project I am co-creating is unfolding at a rapid rate. The lands provide incredible energetic harmony for those who I am synergizing with. I cook on open fires, cleanse in the waters, walk barefoot on the earth and connect daily to the elementals that support all of life. I have little to no use for social media, mainstream media and limit my technology use to what serves me. The search externally for meaning has lost its grip. The meaning of a guru is someone who transmuted the darkness to the light, and I'm well on my way.

All this feels like a stepping stone to a much bigger dream to co-create. The intention for this project is to align with core team members who share a larger dream to cultivate an intentional off grid regenerative farming community. A 500 acre plot of land with sacred temples, communal gardens, animal sanctuaries to be cultivated in tandem with the wisdom keepers of turtle island(canada). A dream I have no doubt will unfold in the near future.

My life has become filled with purpose. The sense of emptiness has alchemized to fulfillment and I feel more vibrant and alive than ever before. The veil is being lifted for those who choose to see the depth of manipulation of consciousness from the hands of the industrial ruling class. Tell-a-vision has programmed beings to live in a state of fear. It's high time we took off the blinders and recognized the god-like abilities we hold as human beings. There is nothing that cannot be achieved if we act cooperatively as one. The threads of outdated socio/political systems are becoming unravelled and the stripping of our liberties for those who stand for pro choice over what foreign elements go into our bodies are pushing we, the people, together to create new paradigms of living that is rooted in value systems of co-creation, love, unity, strength and resilience. Diamonds are formed from incredible amounts of pressure and heat and I choose to think this is what's happening to the collective. Humanity is going through a deep time of renewal and it's high time we reclaim our sovereignty. We have dreamt this reality into existence, giving our powers to the industrial ruling class, I think, to re-awaken us to the incredible gifts, god-like abilities we embody as humans. Power is formed by what we, the people, consent to. It's high time to take back our powers and refrain from participating in systems that are aimed at serving the ruling class. What dream are you a stand to live in?

My life's mission has shifted from living a life of service to just being love and being a warrior to eradicate anything that is not of truth and love.I choose to take in less through the brain, and consciously cultivate deeper states of stillness to connect to the energies of the cosmos, mother earth and to my heart. I have had to face my darkest shadows and bring an incredible amount of forgiveness to myself, to humanity and others. Forgiving myself for getting involved in narcotics and the harm it causes to others. Plant medicine has helped access some of the deepest levels of pain and suffering and have had numerous experiences with Jeshua/Christ supporting me on this path. There is no more time to blame anyone, we must step into radical self responsibility for humanity to thrive. Let go of all the pain and suffering. Let it all go.

It takes conviction to be utterly courageous and follow the path that your soul needs to walk. Sacrifice does not come easily. In order to clear the space to reconnect to source, my heart, and my purpose, I have let go of loved ones, habits, and lifestyles that no longer work. I've been doing the interior wedding of my garden. I embrace stepping into my fullest potential as a human being which is absolutely limitless. Everything I've been through, I feel, has conditioned me to contribute my energies to a new ascended living on planet earth. The winds of change are blowing. We are living through the most highly prophesied time and it's inevitable we return to a time of peace, harmony and love. The transfer of power is unfolding at an alarming rate. Crypto currency is helping to decentralize banking systems which keep us enslaved. Free energy exists here and now, technology that liberates and enhances quality of life can no longer be repressed. The awakening is being propagated at an increasingly rapid pace. The transfer of balance from the mind to the heart is an ongoing process. My biggest fear is not that I'm not good enough. It's that I'm powerful beyond my wildest recognition. It's time to step fully into the fear with absolute faith and conviction of how deeply supported I am. I see now that I have been every step of the way.

Where does this journey lead? Remains to be seen but I do recognize I didn't get Bob Marley and Tupac Shakur tattooed on my chest to sit in silence too long. I swim naked daily in waters, I walk this earth barefoot with rarely a shirt on, nevermind trying to get me wearing a mask. The wild man in me is no longer dormant. I wave at the snowmobiles going by as I meditate beneath the ice surface in the winter. I fell trees on the lake and dance naked around the fire in deep snow. I'm incredibly grateful for the depth of disconnection I've experienced and for the resilience to come out the other side and come back home to mother earth.The mind attacks still come, putting self down, not good enough dialogue, but I know now it is not me. I have the tools to breath through it all. I don't need to punch a clock and live some mundane life and I'm super grateful for that.

ABOUT THE AUTHOR

RANIN-RAWA

Government Name: Geoff, Larden
Spiritual Name: Ranin-Rawa
Cosmic cowboy, land steward and warrior for peace and love in the galaxy

Social media
Instagram:@larden_geoff
Facebook: Geoff Larden

7

TIMOTHY ALEXANDER
TIME TO RISE

I grabbed him by the back of the shirt as he turned and reached for the riffle. It tore away and he got a hold of it. I had no time to think, little time to react and just jumped on him smothering his arms and the riffle. Had he been any stronger he would easily have rolled me off enabling him to shoot me. There was no holding back at this point, I used everything in my power, punches, elbows my own head against his to pry his hand and handcuff him.

His only words to me as I walked him to my police car were, "You're lucky". Even his brother who had visited him, later told me that he would have killed me had he been able to. I didn't at any point feel fear. I had really paid no attention to the comments. At no point did I think how to get out of this situation. I was highly trained by a highly regarded police academy. I had over ten years of intense martial arts training. I just did what I had to do. No thoughts required.

It would be many, many years later that I would reflect and consider the times I had placed myself in a life-threatening situation.

Fourteen years as a police officer, five years as a peace officer. Nine years as a disaster relief manager. Multiple incidents where I was placed at high risk. Where my life could have been taken. Three natural disasters including Canada's worse. All had taken a toll, I had just not realized it.

Nothing, nothing I could ever imagine prepared me for that day in late 2020. The day my wife decided she was leaving me. It cut like a knife through my chest. Pain like I honestly had never felt. My head swirled, emotions swept through me. Every emotion you can imagine from confusion to anger to disgrace and shame.

That first month was topsy turvy to say the least. I'm sure many of you can relate. But this isn't about a failed relationship. It's about trauma that so many of us face throughout our lives. It's about how it affects us negatively. How it can bring us to our darkest places. How our perspectives can change.

More importantly, this is about survival, change, growth, a rebirth. Finding oneself, meaning and purpose. Remember that word, purpose. I'm going to tell you that whatever challenge you are facing. Whether it be your failed relationship, your dwindling finances, your weight gain and suffering health, or you've lost your path in understanding why you are here. There is a solution. There is an answer. There is light through the tunnel.

Go back three years. The darkest place in my mind did not think the next day would be brighter. There was no reasoning. No happy thoughts. No words anyone could say that would bring me around. I just sank deeper and deeper. Anxiety that would make me literally shake uncontrollably. A pit in my stomach that ached. Tears that would run down my face without any reason. Not just sleepless nights, but nights of pacing, aimless driving. Tired, exhausted, but never drifting off to dream land. And if I did happen to for even a couple of hours, those hours were filled with nightmares so vivid, so real, it would scare me from wanting to fall asleep again.

The sight of a man twisted and tangled in a car wreck, trapped and unable to move while his best friend lies lifeless is not something at the time, evoked any emotion in me. I was the consummate professional. I had a job to do. I was alone with him patiently waiting for fire rescue, hydro to shut power off, and the ambulance. I could calm him. I could talk with him. Conversation like where I had met someone in a grocery store in a lineup. We chatted while we waited because there was nothing I could do.

We talked about what he had been doing earlier. About his family. Things he liked to do in his spare time. A golfer like me. I could usually find something in common to discuss with anyone. Ah relief arrived and although the passenger would have to deal with the death of his best friend, he would be ok. Ten minutes later one of the paramedics came over to tell me that he too had passed. And just like so many other incidents similar, or worse than this I just moved along. Next call, next issue, next fight, next domestic, next accident, next death. It became common, almost normal. I didn't even cry at funerals of those I was or had been close with.

For nearly one month after the news last November, I was a lost soul. Not dead, just lost. And that's ok. It's ok to stop, to ponder, to think, rethink, rehash every moment. It's ok to sort things out in your head, to let your mind wonder aimlessly. At least that's what I did. I am thankful that I had at least that one person I could say anything to. I could talk, I could swear, shout, vent, and now I could cry.

Decisions, and transition. Through that month, I knew that everything would be ok. I knew that I would rise again to be myself, better than I was. Knowing that deep down I had a future, didn't make it any less painful, but where there is hope, there is a way. One day I awoke, and something was different. A sense, a feeling, a calmness came over me. It was time!

I had seen a lot, done a lot, experienced a lot during the past thirty years. Things that were not as bad as many had but things nobody should really have to go through. They play out like a horror movie in my head. I can't watch anything with blood and gore. It has affected my short-term memory quite severely. But my long-term memory holds strong. One of those memories is of my police training when I played rugby for the academy team. My first time playing rugby. Definitely one of the toughest sports I've participated in. I remember our coach, and drill instructor telling us at the one and only tournament we participated in that although we may not have known the game very well, we had one great advantage. We were fit, we were strong. A dozen young men most of whom had never played before finished second. That morning I woke with that different sense, I drew upon those words and that tournament.

The decision was made at that moment while lying there contemplating that rugby tournament. Time to rise. There were four pillars that I deemed areas I needed to improve and grow to survive. First was my spiritual being, second my emotional, mental health needed to heal, third my physical self, and last was my financial state.

I didn't set out to just hope something would get better in these areas. I focused all my effort, all my thoughts, all my resources, all my energy. I set a goal, ninety days to a new me. I wrote ideas, and the more I wrote, the more came to me. Piece by piece things slowly began to come together. Little did I know that the fifth element, or pillar, that I had intentionally left out, would become my most important, relationships.

The relationship pillar had been deliberately negated directly because of my failed past. I began going through my list of contacts. I connected with people, four that would become integral parts of my life. Three young women, barely in their 30s, and a close guy friend who would become a brother. Each of them gave to me in ways that I never would have expected. Never would I have dreamed. As a result, I soon came to realize the importance of relationships and added it.

I am gentle with people. I'll say to wade in, or you don't have to do it all at once. I didn't take my own advice. I was determined that in a short ninety days I would make the necessary changes to move my life forward.

I did what I knew best first. There was no initial plan. I heeded the words of Nike and just did it. I began walking daily for an hour. Fitness has always been my friend. I also remembered the words of my martial arts masters, work the body to work the mind. I took that literally and seriously. I joined a gym and trained daily having studied two coaches whose regimens I admired. I bought their programs, wrote out what I needed to do blending both, taking what I believed was the best from each. I knew that exercise, at least for me, would be a pathway to healing, as it had in my past. Although it was now December and the onset of winter here, it didn't matter. I walked and walked. Rain, shine, snow, minus twenty. Even through the December holidays I walked. Even while I traveled to visit family and friends, I walked. When I couldn't lift weights, I trained with my own body weight.

Slowly and surely my physique began to change but even more importantly, my mindset began to change. My perspective began to change. I began to see myself, my true self again. I was asked to join a group of men, totally unexpected and by a total stranger, to complete a seventy-five day challenge. My workouts became more intense, my meal plan shifted to healthier, and I began drinking water, a lot of water. Although I only completed sixty-three days of the challenge, it set me up for lifestyle changes that would become habit. Eight months later I've found new ways to train, and I am in the best shape I have been since age twenty-five. I'm leaner, I'm faster, I look better. I feel better. From 199 pounds to 165 currently.

I was told at a young age and something I have never forgotten that the mind is a powerful thing that is never fully utilized. It controls pain. The body responds to what the mind believes. Therefore, if you believe there is no pain, there isn't.

In the late 80s I competed at my first National Karate Championships. I believe I was twenty-three years old. My first fight was against a tall, experienced fighter. It took him less than a minute to break my nose. Blood spued, my eyes swelled, and blackened. I had limited visibility. But all I could remember were those words, there is no pain. I kept fighting and won that match. My second match I lost to a younger competitor who would actually went onto win the title.

Walking on some days hurt. My knees hurt. Especially the right one. So bad I could barely walk. Injuries from when I was younger. Torn meniscus. It didn't stop me. Walking became my meditation. I know I'll scare some you with that word but bear with me. I grew up when men weren't supposed to show emotions. If you fell, you got up brushed yourself off and went on. My policing career was similar. Be professional, service to your community. I kept walking. Walking along gave me free time. Time to think. Time to decipher things. To put my thoughts into some sort of logical story that made sense and not just a ball of confusion. It allowed me to focus on the steps, the beat I kept. To repeatedly tell myself that it wasn't actually cold out. I allowed me to reflect on what I had read earlier or the night before. On the affirmations I had written out. Walking was healthy, the meditation aspect did wonders for my mental state.

So less than two months after I had received the news of my marriage ending I had put into motion certain things that would change my life in 2021. I had fitness coaches, a personal development coach and mentors, a marketing guru coach and mentors, a spiritual guide, and the financial thing, I thought to myself would figure itself out. Each guiding me, enlightening me, and teaching me and providing the tools for me to succeed.

I read, I watched videos, I sat in on webinars. I was in bed by 1030 pm nightly, and up at 430 am daily. I set up I a routine and scheduled my days.

"Thinking will not overcome fear but action will" W Clement Stone

I just did whatever I was asked of me. If one of my coaches asked how many calls I would make and I said 10, or 20 or more, I did 10, 20 or more. Everything became incredible from that point. Was everything and everyday perfect and filled with fun, friends and good times? Absolutely not. There would be setbacks and more failures. But all along the way, no matter what was thrown at me, my path became more clearly defined. I, for the first time in my life, found purpose.

I found that thing I had heard of so many times, just never understood it.

We are all going to face trauma in one form or another at some point in our lives. Be prepared.

From the time I was a young boy there was something I knew. I remember giving a short reading of something when I was around seven years old to a large audience. It was then I knew there was something greater in store for me. That I was placed here to do something more than exist.

Today I try to keep my life simple. Simple things, simple rules. Especially when faced with those experiences that can have detrimental effects.

I do what I know best. If that time, when that time happens again, I'll exercise even more. I will lift more, walk more.

I'll continue to surround myself with amazing people. Your true friends will rise. You'll be challenged by them, but genuinely loved along the way.

Daily, I think of my purpose. What I am doing that day and does it align with my purpose. I think of where my energy is going and keep it flowing guided by my inner being.

I read and listen, daily. I once heard that our brains need a good washing daily to clean up the crap we are fed.

I try to be kind. To spread love. Doesn't matter what else is going on, who else agrees or not. I give from my heart, of myself and all I have.

I continue to meet new people. Develop new interests. As a result there are always new opportunities.

I keep learning about my personal spirituality. Each and every one of us gives off a vibe, an energy. Like minds, like energies, and vibes flow to each other.

"Whether you think you can or think you can't you're right" Henry Ford

ABOUT THE AUTHOR
TIMOTHY ALEXANDER

Born May 1965 in Newfoundland and Labrador, Canada. Sports were his first love. Raised in a Middle Class household to the most amazing and above average parents and one brother. Although he attended three years of university, school just never sat right in his head and at twenty-five quit and joined the Royal Canadian Mounted Police.

Fourteen years of police service and thousands of life experiences would bring him to private business and independence. An entrepreneur at heart and still to this day. He has found purpose through difficult times and willingly shares knowledge gained through the years.

Today he lives in Kelowna, British Columbia, Canada, a valley surrounded by beautiful mountains, lakes and takes full advantage of the outdoors, sunshine, amazing views and the multitude of amenities and activities.

From a young age he was called to serve in a greater capacity and at a higher level. He now commits himself to personal development, and a focus on spirituality, mental, emotional health, financial well being and physical fitness and to that for others.

ZACHARY HARDING

FROM DJ TO CEO – A GUIDE TO BETTER DECISION-MAKING SKILLS

"Do it for the Love, not the Likes" - Chronixx

In his song Exodus, Bob Marley sings: "OPEN your eyes, look within, are you satisfied with the life you're living?" But let's remix that a little. I am going to ask you instead to CLOSE your eyes and look within, (I mean give it a try, put the book down for a second) and then ask yourself are you feeling fulfilled by the life you're living?

Anyone reading this who is truly fulfilled by the life you are currently living can skip this chapter, because you've already figured life out. If you continue reading, this means there is still an opportunity for further personal growth and development.

In the daytime, I'm the founder and CEO of Delta Capital Partners, a private equity firm based in Kingston, Jamaica. But by night, I'm a DJ.

They call me the Dancehall CEO.

What is Dancehall? Dancehall is Jamaica's urban music and subculture which you've probably enjoyed before without even realising it.

If you've ever listened to music from recording artistes like Sean Paul, Shaggy, Damian Marley, Beenie Man, or Bounty Killa, then you know what dancehall is. Or you may know the genre by another name. Dancehall has been adopted by other cultures under names like Reggaeton, or Ragga and has even been heavily incorporated into Pop, Hip Hop, and Afro Beats. In earlier times dancehall artistes were often added to spice up the hook of a pop song such as Lady Saw featured on the pop track "Smile" by Vitamin C, or Bounty Killa on "Hey Baby" by the legendary punk/ska act No Doubt. Today, thankfully the sound is being recognized in its own right, and songs like Justin Bieber's "Sorry" and Drake's "Controller" are undeniably set to dancehall rhythms.

Dancehall is ingrained in my DNA and has been a catalyst for many of my major life moments both personally and professionally. The passion and raw emotion of the music have served as my "True North." In fact, back in the late 90s into the early 2000s I was Sean Paul's first manager, before my brother Jeremy Harding took over and managed him through to milestones like winning a Grammy among other global awards and selling over a million records to achieve RIAA Platinum certification. In addition to being Sean's first manager, I co-founded a dancehall record label with Jeremy who also produced Beenie Man's monster hit "Who Am I", (also known by its popular hook "Sim Simma") on our 2Hard Records label.

The Jamaican dancehall scene is wild, passionate, stylish and sexy. A party, also known as a *"dance"* or *"session"* as we call it, represents unbridled freedom and fun wrapped up in one bundle. The music reflects the experiences, perspectives, and general attitudes of contemporary Jamaicans. It is a way of life and influences every part of our culture and language.

Even the Prime Minister of Jamaica, the Most Honourable Andrew Holness, has a dancehall nickname. He is affectionately known as "The Most Honourable BroGad" - slang from a dancehall song which means that he's THE Boss.

In our last national political elections, members of parliament were even competing over who had the coolest dancehall battle song as their theme song for campaigning.

While it may seem surprising to some that a gritty urban art form has taken on such an elevated role, the genre has influenced the world in areas such as entertainment, sport, and fashion. For me, dancehall has been my *CEO Master Class*. Dancehall is not just music—it's a mindset and has strongly influenced and guided my corporate life.

I started my career as a DJ or as we say in the dancehall a *"Selector"*, and this exposed me to dancehall artistes being more than musicians, but rather contemporary philosophers, who can distill complex concepts into words, sound, movement, and trends.

Being a DJ programmed me to think differently. As a result, I've developed a formula for decision-making that I think anyone can use to make more fulfilling business and life decisions—like a boss.

My corporate career began in Marketing and for several years I had great success helping several brands and companies to grow exponentially and even helped turn some of these brands into household names in Jamaica.

I never really stopped to think why things were working out so well for me at the time or even about how I was doing it. I had just married my wife Tamara, and had two young daughters—Tori and Zara—so I was highly driven. I was working around the clock trying to provide for my family.

One day, a prominent journalist asked me, "What's your secret to successful decision making?" I had never thought about it before nor considered its role in my life on an ideological or on a professional level. I paused and then the answer came to me in an epiphany.

I said, "IT'S FROM BEING A DJ!"

The connection between marketing and spinning tracks is not an obvious one, but the experience of being a DJ actually has strong parallels to marketing strategy if you dissect it. You see as a DJ, you have to continuously read the target market: (a.k.a. the crowd), in order to present the right product: (the song), to elicit a purchase decision or buy-in: (such as singing out, dancing, or putting your hands in the air).

Now, the goal of getting a crowd reaction is fairly similar for DJs across genres. You need to be able to change the energy of the crowd in a split-second. The crowd doesn't know or care about how you do it. They don't understand the process of beat-matching, cutting, scratching mixing or using effects to transition (all nerdy DJ stuff). The only thing that matters to them is how they feel based on what they're hearing. That's it. The end result is what you are judged on.

But in the Dancehall arena, it's even more serious. The crowd has ultimate veto-power. If the DJ isn't in top form, the crowd will very passionately and sometimes aggressively boo them off the stage. It's the same pressure you face as a CEO, except it is much more intense as you have money and people's livelihoods at stake. If you are a bad leader and poor decision-maker, you won't last very long on the corporate stage.

In my daily professional life, I must be able to make the right decisions, in real-time, to keep winning the hearts and souls of our investors, our portfolio companies and the customers and consumers of our products and services.

This leads me to the big question:

"HOW do I consistently make the best decisions?"

Well, this question is obviously subjective. The best decision has to be the best decision for most if not all stakeholders involved, and of course it has to be the best decision for me too. With so much to consider, there's a lot to account for in the decision-making process.

This new theory I am proposing presents a sequence of steps designed to help you make decisions that lead will lead to more fulfilling outcomes in your life. So, let's take a look at what I am calling the CARE-FUL decision-making formula. The name is meant to indicate that decisions made with C.A.R.E. should leave you feeling more FULfilled.

The acronym for the formula is C-A-R-E.
C is for CROSSROADS
A is for AUTHENTICITY
R is for RISK, and
E is for EMOTION.

Let's break it down.

It all starts with recognizing when you're at a **Crossroads** and that you have options in trying to make the best decision.

The most powerful tool in life is being aware and deliberate about when and how you want to make changes in your life. This includes being conscious of your decision points, choosing to make a decision, and knowing what the expected outcome should be.

As humans, we usually don't like change. In fact, we're often afraid of it - even when it might be to our benefit. If I were to say that everyone who adopts this new Decision-Making Model over the next 24 hours will completely change their lives forever, some of you might try it, but honestly, most wouldn't give it a second thought. It is no secret that people fight change. Whether consciously or not, most of us might think we want to change but when it comes down to it, we don't want to try anything new. Even when it hurts or doesn't get us anywhere, we are wired to stick to what we're accustomed to.

The reason so many people feel unsatisfied, unfulfilled, and unable to grow, is because they don't make decisions in a deliberate or structured way. Our decisions determine who we are and how far we can go, and yet the vast majority of us are adamant that the "hit or miss" formula we've been using to make decisions for far too long, will lead us to the right place. If that were true, you wouldn't be reading this book.

Amelia Earhart said, "The most difficult thing is the decision to ACT. The rest is merely tenacity. You can do anything you decide to do. You can act to change and control your life."

But I understand this concept much better from the streets of Kingston or "Dancehall University" in the form of lyrics from dancehall artist Sizzla Kolanji's song, 'Rise to the Occasion', which says:

"Rise to the occasion look at yourself then say you're strong, no one can stop you.

Rise to the occasion go ahead u know you're strong, no one can stop you.

It's for you to make the best in life, know that you've got the chance.

Get up and step to towards your goal, it's alright - fulfill your needs and wants"

Both these ideas highlight the significance of coming to a Crossroads.

Decisions don't always have to be daunting. Today you made several decisions before you picked up this book. You had to choose where to sit, what kind of lighting you need, when to start reading, etc. I guarantee right now someone reading this is even thinking, should I grab a snack before really diving deeper into this chapter?

Some of these decisions are easy because we've been taught HOW to make them, and we have considerable experience in making them. In fact, we make 90% of our choices subconsciously.

However, for bigger decisions, such as those that have the potential to change the trajectory of our lives, a lot of us are clueless and we panic, am I right? (I can see you nodding in agreement right now).

To help you consider those decision points, let's go back to the turntables.

A good DJ knows exactly when to drop that beat and when to mix it out. We all have this intuitive sense though; it's not just reserved for DJs. It's a feeling. We all know when something just doesn't feel right and when it is time for a change.

Ask anyone at a party what they thought about the DJ playing and they will tell you, "they played too much of this and not enough of that, or the pace was too fast or too slow." They can just feel it. This same instinct kicks-in when you're at a key decision point in your life. Needing to change a song is not much different from needing to change something in your life!

If your unmet needs are consuming your thoughts, then you are at a Crossroads. You can feel it. So just surrender and know that it's decision time! When you are feeling stuck and frequently find yourself thinking, "I need more of this or I wish I could do some of that", then you know it's time for a change.

In the world of Dancehall, the DJ is accountable for the vibe. In sport, the coach is responsible for the team's performance (just ask any Premier League or Super Bowl coach who has been fired), and in business, the CEO is accountable for the company's performance.

In YOUR life, there is only one person who is responsible for making that final decision and that person is YOU.

You are the CEO of your life!

The next step in my CARE-FUL decision-making formula is **Authenticity**.

People throw this word around a lot but let's be guided by popular professor, author and TED speaker Dr. Brene Brown who says, "Authenticity is the daily practice of letting go of who we think we're supposed to be and embracing who we are."

Chronixx, one of the world's biggest dancehall artistes at the moment, and a personal favourite of mine, explains that maintaining authenticity is the key to successful decision making. He sings:

"Inna dancehall style, a nuh everybody a go like we, but we well Irie, 'cause we nuh love likes."

Meaning, "in the dancehall, not everyone is going to like us, but we are still fine (Irie) because we don't love likes."

He goes on to sing, *"Mi do it fi di love... mi nuh do it fi di likes"* meaning —I do things for the love of it and not only for social media likes. Then, *"success don't come overnight, let them know it's substance over hype. We do it for the love we don't do it for the likes."*

Quite often, others may not support what will make you happy. So, when making authentic decisions, ask yourself how you will feel about it after.

Authentic decisions, regardless of the outcome, tend to lead you toward a more satisfying life. When your decisions are authentic, they guide you to express your true self and move you toward other increasingly clear and authentic decisions.

You don't want to live a life of continuously making the *lesser-of-two-evils* decisions. Whenever this happens check whether your authenticity is in or out of alignment.

So, we've covered C – Crossroads, and A - Authenticity, now on to the tough part R - **Risk.** Risk is a fundamental part of every decision we make. But when we hear risk most people think "What could go wrong?" Well, now that I've designated you as a newly minted DJ, let's remix the Risk, and see what we can learn from a DJ's perspective on Risk, because it is quite different.

From a DJs perspective, risk is actually about calculating the probability of a win. It opens you to the possibility of being admired and respected versus being criticized. So, the remixed question we need to ask ourselves is:

"What could this decision be worth to you?"

You see calculating risk isn't just about what could go wrong, it is about calculating the probability of what could go right. A healthy attitude towards Risk is actually about assessing the potential Reward.

Let's look at another quote by director, Fred Wilcox: "Progress always involves risk; you can't steal second base and keep your foot on first." This is so true. We have to let go of our past doubts and current fears, in order to step into our future success.

Playwright, critic and political activist, George Bernard Shaw said it even better: "The reasonable man adapts himself to the world; the unreasonable one persists in trying to adapt the world to himself. Therefore, all progress depends on the unreasonable man." It is the unreasonable man, the one that changed their circumstances in order to make a meaningful difference who is usually the one who took the biggest risk.

Let that sink in for a bit.

Jamaicans have a questionable understanding of the possible negative outcomes of Risk. We don't think about Risk. We think about Winning. As a small country of approximately three million people, we punch way above our weight class, and I think it has something to do with a particular attitude we call being "boasy," a derivative of boastful, but without the arrogance.

Boasy is a mix of bravado, powered by the ability to back it up. Jamaicans expect that once you've chosen a path, you must execute with a high level of confidence. We refer to this attitude as being "boasy".

As a developing nation, no one expects us to outshine our global counterparts who, fundamentally, have access to more resources. But we continuously do so. We let our minds travel to the farthest extent of the possible Reward. And when we stand to gain a lot, we figure the risk will be worth the reward.

I can't think of a better example of Jamaican "boasyness" than the Honourable Usain St. Leo Bolt.

At his first Olympics in 2004, at age eighteen, Bolt was touted as the next legend of the track; however, he was eliminated in the first round, and at home he was given a really hard time for it. If Bolt had looked at risk as everything that could have gone wrong for his future, he would have given into his injury and accepted the possibility of not being able to rise to the occasion. He would have walked away from sprinting. But when Usain Bolt hears Risk, he gets "boasy". When they questioned how he was doing it – he got "boasy". When they said it was a fluke, and then he went on to win every world title and even reset his own Olympic records and world records, that was the epitome of being "boasy".

So always assess the risks, but look at them also as opportunities to WIN!

You've come to the **Crossroads** with your most **Authentic** self and remixed the **Risk**. Now for the final piece of the puzzle, you must fuel the decision with the right **Emotion.**

You must be Emotionally aligned with your decisions if you want to sustain their outcomes. Ask yourself:
- Are my emotions compatible with my decisions?
- Are the emotions behind my decisions mostly positive or negative?
- What emotional mindset do I need to sustain the outcomes?

For example, if you want to be powerful you have to conquer fear. If you want to be a leader you have to control your anger. And if you want to be influential you may need to practice greater appreciation.

Considering the status of your own emotions as well as the emotions of others around you is at the core of what is called Emotional Intelligence. Why is this crucial? Because being able to manage and control your own emotions in any decision-making situation is your hidden Superpower.

No matter how logical we think we are, we're all emotional beings. Our success depends on navigating our own emotions as well as the emotions of others. This is known as being emotionally intelligent. Understanding this is absolutely critical, because you can't control other people's behaviour; but you can control how you react to their behaviour.

Practicing Emotional Intelligence will not only turn you into a decision-making machine, it will also turn you into an unstoppable magnetic force, capable of attracting all your desires, and manifesting your wildest dreams.

In the dancehall, the DJ is accountable for the vibe and in business, the CEO is accountable for the company's performance. In your life, the only person responsible for making that final decision is you.

My father always used to tell me, "Son, it takes many to deliberate, but one to decide."

Remember: You get to choose your own Theme Song and You get to decide when to drop that Beat.

Make decisions with the vibe of a true dancehall DJ using the C.A.R.E. formula and I believe you'll be well on your way to achieving greater Fulfillment in your life!

ABOUT THE AUTHOR
ZACHARY HARDING

Zachary Harding is Executive Chairman and co-founder of Delta Capital Partners, and Chief Executive Officer (CEO) of the Stocks & Securities Limited (SSL) Group both based in Kingston Jamaica. He is a member of the Forbes Business Council and was also named the 2021 Stockbroker CEO of the Year for Jamaica by the Global Banking & Finance Awards®. Prior to taking the helm of SSL, Harding was founder and Chairman of Hyperion Equity, a private investment firm with holdings in technology, cutting edge entertainment, and infrastructure ventures. Over the years, he developed a stellar track record while in senior positions including CEO, Head of Strategy, and Director of Marketing, among other leadership positions within companies such as Appliance Traders Ltd, Wisynco, Red Stripe (Diageo) and Grace Kennedy Remittance Services Ltd. He was the first CEO of the Caribbean Climate Smart Accelerator, an initiative started by Virgin boss Richard Branson along with three Caribbean Prime Ministers.

In 2012, Harding was named as one of the Top "50-under-Fifty Business Leaders Shaping Jamaica's Future" by the Private Sector Organization of Jamaica and The Gleaner Newspaper. As a venture capitalist Harding invested heavily in the Creative Industry, both funding and producing the documentary "One People" - the official documentary of Jamaica's 50th Anniversary of Independence, as well as the acclaimed feature film "Sprinter". In 2021 he presented the

C.A.R.E-Ful decision-making model, (a proprietary, culture-based structure) at TEDx Aston University.

Harding has been dubbed a "rain-maker" and "marketing guru" based on several ground-breaking campaigns and brand turnarounds. His innovative mind and strategic acumen have led him to be selected as Special Advisor to the Minister of Tourism and Deputy Director at the Jamaica Tourist Board. He is currently appointed by the Minister of Finance to serve as the Government of Jamaica representative on the Board of Caribbean Airlines Ltd., and by the Prime Minister to serve on the board of JAMPRO where he chairs the Projects and Marketing Subcommittee. Previously, he has served on several other boards, including the Port Authority of Jamaica, the Jamaica Manufacturers' Association, the Urban Development Corporation, Jamaica Antidoping Commission, the Sports and Entertainment Network under the Ministry of Tourism where he is deputy chair. He also serves his country as a Justice of the Peace.

Twitter: @zacharding27
Instagram: @zacharding27
LinkedIn: Zachary Harding

ABOUT THE PUBLISHER

Soulfully Aligned Publishing House exists to bring healing, transformation and aligned service through the written word to the world.

Created and founded by Best Selling Author, Sandra Rodriguez Bicknell and Vanessa Ferraro, their mission is to highlight the voices of healers around the world to the mainstream to exemplify the power of having a story, and not being your story. Soulfully Aligned Publishing donates all book proceeds to various charities around the world as chosen by their authors. We are committed to bringing conscious, harmonious principles to the way we operate our business and are here to magnify and empower all whom we work with to align to their Soul, their message and their service to the world.

Made in United States
Orlando, FL
16 October 2022